The World According to
NIGEL FARAGE

The World According to
NIGEL FARAGE

A PARODY BY MARK LEIGH

JOHN BLAKE

Published by John Blake Publishing Ltd,
3 Bramber Court, 2 Bramber Road,
London W14 9PB, England

www.johnblakepublishing.co.uk

www.facebook.com/johnblakebooks
twitter.com/jblakebooks

This edition published in 2015

ISBN: 978 1 78418 599 2

British Library Cataloguing-in-Publication Data:

A catalogue record for this book is available from the British Library.

Design by www.envydesign.co.uk

Printed in Great Britain by CPI Group (UK) Ltd

1 3 5 7 9 10 8 6 4 2

Images used on pp.114–120 and p.247 © Shutterstock
Illustrations by Andrew Pinder

The right of Mark Leigh to be identified as the author of this work has been asserted by him in accordance with the Copyright, Designs and Patents Act 1988.

Papers used by John Blake Publishing are natural, recyclable products made from wood grown in sustainable forests. The manufacturing processes conform to the environmental regulations of the country of origin.

Every attempt has been made to contact the relevant copyright-holders, but some were unobtainable. We would be grateful if the appropriate people could contact us.

Contents

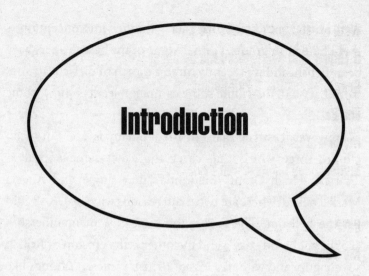

Introduction

Welcome Dear Reader,
I salute* you for buying this book (or graciously accepting it as a gift from a well-meaning friend).

People come up to me and say, 'Nigel, you're a thoroughly decent bloke. Don't you get hacked off because there are so many misconceptions about you and your party?' Well the answer is, 'Too bloody right!', which is why I'm really glad this book will help set the record straight.

The main fallacy is that we're a one-policy party. That's so not true! We have loads of great polices about the NHS, climate change, shale gas, the armed forces, foreign aid, tuition fees etc., but they don't make for good press. I mean, if you're an editor what headline are you going to run with – 'Farage to end burdensome green levy' or 'Farage says foreigners smell'?

And on the subject of foreigners, another misconception is that I hate immigrants. I don't! Some of my best cleaners have been Polish, and we recently hired a bunch of dirt-cheap guys from Latvia to distribute some campaign leaflets (how ironic is that!).

However it is true that our main enemy is The European Union; three words that carry the exact same appeal as 'Starring Hugh Grant', 'Madonna's new single' and 'Angela Merkel naked'. There are two main reasons why the UK should get the hell out. The first is the huge cost of membership (£55m per bloody day!) and the other is the erosion of British sovereignty and with it, a loss of British values. It's things like queuing, nostalgia, niceness, drunkenness, self-loathing and obesity that have made this country what it is today.

In fact I'd go as far as to say I'd rather embrace someone with Ebola before I embraced Europe. In fact, not only should you not embrace Europe, you should actually push it away from you, punch it in the stomach and, as it doubles up, kick it hard in the balls, then deliver a sharp chop to the back of its neck before pulling it down on to the ground and stamping on its greasy, foreign head.

The last time Great Britain went into Europe with any degree of success was on 6 June 1944 and since then things have gone rapidly downhill faster than you can say 'Veto'.

Cheers!

Nigel

---

*A proper military salute, not a Third Reich type of salute, okay?

Is UKIP the Party For You?

You've heard of detailed psychometric tests to assess your personality? Well, this isn't one of them.

The man in the street doesn't have time for all that mumbo-jumbo,* he just wants to get on with his life, do an honest day's work for an honest day's pay and have time for a leisurely pint afterwards. So, taking this test to see if you're compatible with UKIP's ideals won't take long.

Is it scientific? Of course! It's as scientific as the basis for our policies on climate change.

Do you *have* to do it? Don't worry, it's not the law (which is surprising really, since the EU has passed 3,600 new laws since 2010).

Is it easy to do? Definitely! It's as easy as dismissing Danny Alexander's grasp on basic economics.

Just tick the boxes if you agree with the following statements and check your score afterwards.

1. Do you get your worldview from hearsay, conjecture and the *Mail Online*? ☐

2. Is your first reaction to really heavy rainfall, 'That's God's punishment for same-sex marriages'? ☐

3. Do you ever let prejudice, selfishness and fear cloud your judgement? ☐

4. Does hearing the following words or phrases make you feel uncomfortable and apprehensive: *savoir-faire, zeitgeist, piazza, polski sklep*? ☐

5. When you see subtitled speech on a foreign film do you immediately think, 'I wonder what they're *really* saying?' ☐

6. Does being 'hot in bed' usually involve an electric blanket? ☐

7. When someone mentions the European Court of Human Rights, do you automatically want to punch them in the face? ☐

8. Do you believe that all Romanians are vampires? ☐

9. Is your Sky+ box filled with repeats of *Top Gear*,
    Time Team and *Dad's Army*?

10. Do you paint St George's Cross on your face even
    when England aren't playing?

11. Do you blame your poor sexual performance on
    your anxiety at not being able to live up to the
    reputations of the French and Italians as better
    lovers?

12. Do you think that political correctness is ridiculous
    and we should be allowed to call a spade a spade,
    and the long-term unemployed a parasitic
    underclass?

13. Do you think that our foreign aid budget should be
    reduced to a level where it pays for just 2,000 sacks
    of rice and 400 bottles of fizzy water?

14. When you hear the phrase 'Alice in Wonderland' do
    you immediately think of the 1865 novel written
    by English author Lewis Carroll rather than our
    economic policies?

15. Do you place Theme Pubs in the same category as
    fanatical terrorism?

RESULTS

11-15

Congratulations! You're just what we're looking for: someone who really feels uncomfortable with foreigners, minority groups and reason, and for whom a warm pint, a caravan holiday and fanatical jingoism sum up what's truly great about our incredible nation.

6-10

Not bad. You demonstrate a reasonable level of intolerance but you need to spend a bit more time talking to taxi drivers, working-class blokes in your local or anyone who has a Union Jack tattoo on his neck to get a more complete appreciation of our policies.

5 or less

Sod off and join the Tories, the Lib. Dems. or Labour. Or if you have absolutely no self-esteem, the Greens.

*Incidentally, don't confuse 'mumbo-jumbo' with Bongo Bongo Land.

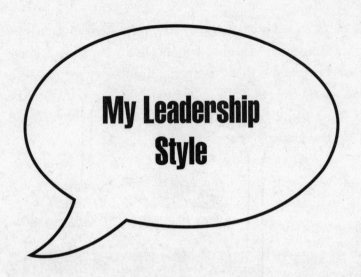

My Leadership Style

I've been accused of being lots of things.

Misogynistic, racist, chauvinistic, intolerant, bigoted, a fascist, blinkered and a bullying dictator.

I absolutely deplore these constant attacks on my character and will state once more for the record that I am not misogynistic, racist, chauvinistic, intolerant, bigoted, a fascist or blinkered.

I do however admit that my leadership style can polarise people.

There are party members who welcome it and there are some who don't – and quite frankly, as far as I'm concerned, those people can just piss off and leave UKIP. Bloody whingers.

A party like mine, I mean *ours*, needs a strong hand on the rudder.

As a working MEP gearing up for a general election I have

THE WORLD ACCORDING TO NIGEL FARAGE

enough on my plate without having to deal with anyone questioning my decisions in public. In my book that's worse than being disobedient: it's being disloyal. I can deal with that easily enough by persuading the dissenters that maybe it's time to grab their coats, say goodbye to the host (me) and leave this particular party.

But what annoys me the most is when some of my so-called colleagues accuse me of running the party like Stalin. That's absolutely bloody nonsense. I am so not like Stalin! Just look at the differences between us:

	JOSEPH STALIN	ME
Reputation	Evil dictator	Conviction politician
Political position	General Secretary of the Central Committee of the Communist Party of the Soviet Union	MEP
Number of deaths responsible for	23.9 million	0*
Famines responsible for	Ukrainian	None. Although at a policy discussion meeting I once told Godfrey Bloom that he couldn't have any more biscuits.
Name of best known initiative	The Great Purge	Leaving the EU

	JOSEPH STALIN	ME
Nickname given to him by the press	Father of Nations	Fruitcake
Portrayal by the press	Beloved, wise, caring yet strong father figure, with the Soviet populace as his children.	Charismatic fascist
Songs written about him	'Hymn to Stalin' by A. V. Avidenko (1936)	'UKIP Calypso' by Mike Read (2014)
Method of dealing with criticism	Exile to the Gulag or execution	Calling it 'laughable nonsense'
Number of blockades instigated against Berlin	1	0*
Close friends with	Mao Tse-tung and Kim il-Sung	Mike Read

*at time of going to press

At the Movies

Apart from smoking, drinking and more smoking and drinking, one of my favourite ways to unwind is by going to the cinema. I get so enraged though when I've parted with a king's ransom for the ticket and eagerly sit back awaiting the start of the film, only to discover that it bears absolutely no resemblance to what I anticipated.

I'm a firm believer that films should have titles that clearly tell you what they're about.

I mean, if you saw a poster for *Dumb and Dumber* you'd assume it was a biopic about David Cameron and Nick Clegg... but it actually isn't. And how was I to know that *The Full Monty* was about male strippers, not an affectionate retrospective about Field Marshal Bernard Montgomery, one of this country's best military leaders?

I tell you, the money I've wasted on being conned like this

is no one's business – and to ensure you don't fall into the same trap I've put this guide together, so people who think like me don't get fooled again.

My Guide to Movies with Confusing Titles

Angela's Ashes
I got in a right row with the cinema manager over this one. I was really looking forward to seeing a film where the German Chancellor gets sealed alive in a coffin, which is then really slowly fed into a crematorium. Instead I got some drivel about an Irish family trying to escape the poverty of pre-war Limerick. Very disappointing!

No Country for Old Men
I'd been waiting for ages for a social documentary about the dire economic consequences of allowing elderly immigrants into the UK. This was not it.

Unforgiven
To my frustration this was not a film about Edward Heath selling out the United Kingdom's sovereignty in 1973, but a story about a retired Wild West gunslinger.

The Beach
I was expecting an accurate portrayal of the Normandy landings. I didn't get one. Okay, there was a beach but it was

severely lacking in amphibious landing vehicles or Panzer IV tanks. And Leonardo DiCaprio did not look anything like General Dwight D. Eisenhower.

The Bourne Supremacy

I love this quaint Lincolnshire market town, which incidentally was the birthplace of Hereward the Wake, the brave resistance leader who led the rebellion against the Norman conquest of England, but this film was less travelogue and more CIA spy thriller. Not quite what I had in mind.

Shane

It was with huge anticipation that I waited for this documentary about probably the greatest Australian fast bowler. All I got though was a film about cowboys, settlers and a cattle owner. It was rubbish.

Monty Python's Life of Brian

If I was annoyed with *Shane* then I almost blew a gasket after sitting through what I thought would be a film about the legendary cricket commentator Brian Johnston. I walked out before the end so I don't actually know if he made an appearance or not (I don't think he did).

Das Boot

It's about a German submarine not sensible footwear. Don't bother!

The Good, the Bad and the Ugly

Although a documentary ostensibly about girl groups doesn't really appeal to me, I recommended it to my niece, thinking the title meant it was about the Bangles, Girls Aloud and Little Mix. She was very annoyed she'd wasted good money on a film about three bounty-hunting cowboys.

Rain Man

I got Dustin Hoffman. I expected Michael Fish.

Liar Liar

If you were expecting an informative documentary about the myth of man-made climate change you'll be sorely frustrated. I know I was. This film's actually about a lawyer who has to tell the truth for 24 hours (as if that would happen!).

There's Something About Mary

I love English history and I'm a big fan of the Tudor period. Mary Queen of Scots is a character that has long fascinated me. However this film didn't make any sense whatsoever. There was nothing about her time with the French Court or the murder of Lord Darnley – let alone her tragic beheading. There was a scene about hair gel but I couldn't see the relevance of this at all.

Titanic

I keep asking myself: how many times can I be misled?! This was a film about the ill-fated ocean liner, and not an insightful documentary about the Greek debt crisis.

Lethal Weapon

As a fan of WW2 militaria and in particular British armoured fighting vehicles, I was looking forward to a film about the Cruiser Tank Mk VIII, or the Cromwell, as it was known. In the end I got a buddy movie about two policemen.

How to Lose Friends and Alienate People

Less a story about Ed Miliband becoming leader of the Labour Party in 2010 and more a tale about a British writer struggling to fit in at a high-profile magazine in New York. Lots of back-stabbing though, so I guess it wasn't totally dissimilar.

Coma

I was convinced this film was going to be a satirical look at life in Luxembourg. I wasn't prepared for a hospital-based conspiracy film. Scary (though not as scary as spending more than 24 hours in Luxembourg).

Alien

Instead of a film about an asylum seeker from North Africa I got a story about an evil stowaway that has to be destroyed at all costs. Close enough.

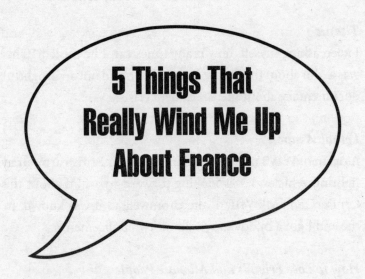

5 Things That Really Wind Me Up About France

France truly is a land of contrasts. Take Paris for example. Everything unpleasant about France is exacerbated in the capital; it's difficult to think of inhabitants of a city who are more snobbish or condescending. Then there's Marseilles which offers visitors everything they'd associate with a bustling cosmopolitan port: racial tension, street crime, low-level drug dealers, rife alcoholism, cheap prostitutes, gang fights and police on the take. As for Provence… well, with forests, olive groves, medieval hilltop villages, smelly food markets and artistic glassware you'll be bored to tears after a few hours, let alone a whole year.

Given that British visitors are generally resented and treated like *merde*, it's a wonder why anyone would ever want to go there in the first place.

As it's often said, the best thing between England and France is the sea.

1. The French are so damn rude!
But don't just take my word for it. French rudeness is there for all to see and hear in different ways. Take the Gallic shrug for example: this was invented by the French as a way to say 'Up yours' because they were too lazy to speak. Then there's the French custom of pretending not to understand English when they so obviously do (a habit often accompanied by the Gallic shrug).

2. …and arrogant
They may have invented the word *grandeur* but they also have delusions of it. Not only do the French call their country La Grande Nation, but they also chose the cock as their national emblem. What's more, they truly believe they invented not just the guillotine and the bidet but also food, wine, sex and fashion. This arrogance manifests itself in most French men thinking they're God's gift to women and most French women thinking they're God's gift to fashion designers. It's no surprise then, to learn that Horace Walpole, the 4th Earl of Orford, described the French as having 'insolent and unfounded airs of superiority'.

3. French music is as derivative as it is atrocious
Surprisingly for a country that has always encouraged and supported the arts, the French music scene hasn't just failed

to develop and evolve, it's actually moved backwards. If you want to know what's hot in the French music scene just cast your mind back to what was popular here fifteen years ago and you'll hear a pale imitation of it nowadays on French radio and TV. Flick through the channels and you'll see the Backstreet Boys topping the charts and a host of Prince and Spice Girls tribute acts. The biggest French music star, however, is Johnny Halliday, a 72-year-old known as the 'French Elvis' but who has aspirations to resemble Johnny Depp. Better known for his plastic surgery than any discernible talent.

4. Everyone moans

And I don't mean in some sort of a sexy Jane Birkin way. I mean the French are never happier than when they're complaining about someone or something. It started in 1789 and the tradition is alive and well today. They'll strike and blockade roads or ports at the drop of a *chapeau* while protests, demonstrations and other acts of civil disobedience are as natural to the French as their cavalier attitude towards personal hygiene. Even their most famous son Napoleon once commented, 'The French complain of everything, and always.'

5. Napoleon is bloody everywhere

You can understand celebrating Richard the Lionheart, Lord Nelson or Winston Churchill. These were truly great and inspirational leaders – but most obviously of all, they were victorious. When it comes to the French, however, the person they hold in the highest esteem is a failed French dictator and megalomaniac. Over two hundred French streets, institutions and monuments celebrate a man whose greatest legacy was not on the battlefield, but in lending his name to a psychological phenomenon involving aggressive behaviour in weedy, short men.

---

3 Useful Phrases to Use in France

How many different types of cheese do you actually need?
Combien de types de fromage vous réellement besoin?

I am aware that Albert Camus said, 'I know of only one duty, and that is to love', but that does not give you the automatic right to put your hand on my wife's bottom.
Je suis conscient que Albert Camus dit: «Je ne connais qu'un seul devoir, et ce est d'aimer», mais cela ne vous donne pas automatiquement le droit de mettre la main sur les fesses de ma femme.

Thank you for asking but I do not want to purchase a beret. Why would I want any headwear that is modelled on a cowpat?
Merci de demander mais je ne veux pas acheter un béret. Pourquoi voudrais-je tout couvre-chef qui est calqué sur une bouse de vache?

**Breastfeeding in Public.
Just Say No.**

Look, there seems to be a lot of confusion lately about our policy towards breastfeeding in public.

The first thing to note is that UKIP doesn't actually have a policy on breastfeeding in public. Policies on controlled immigration, foreign aid and bespoke trade agreements, yes, but breastfeeding, no. I mean, that would be ridiculous; it would be like us having a policy on limiting the number of foreign players in British football teams, which we don't, by the way. Yet.

Anyway, what happened was that I made some remarks during a radio interview about breastfeeding after a posh London hotel told a mother having tea there to cover up. Afterwards I got called a brute and a dinosaur by the growing lobby of breastfeeding fascists. Yes, that's a strong term I know, but I'm comfortable using it since I know a thing or two about fascists.

I'm not some fuddy duddy who feels awkward about seeing breasts. Look, I'm the first one to shout, 'Tits out for the lads!' at closing time. What I am against, however is breastfeeding in public.

Like having children called Zebedee and Artemis, making your own pesto and watching foreign-language films on purpose, breastfeeding in public (or 'attachment parenting' as they pretentiously call it) is a middle-class affectation.

The Motherhood Mafia say 'Breast is best'.

'No it's bloody not!' I say.

10 Reasons Why Breastfeeding in Public is Wrong

1. Have you heard of the phrase 'indecent exposure'? If a man flashed in public, especially that close to a baby, he'd be Tasered before you could say 'exhibitionism'. You can't have one rule for each gender; this isn't Saudi Arabia, you know.
2. Children are meant to be seen and not heard. If you're rude enough to take a screaming brat to a public eatery and ruin the ambience for everyone else, then at least have the decency to leave the table to feed it. And don't worry; no one will steal your poncey macchiato when you're away from your table for a few minutes.

3. Women who flash their breasts and nipples in public are just wanton attention seekers.

4. Or are desperately trying to attract other men.

5. No one really wants to see blue-veined, bloated, milk-engorged lumpy bosoms while they're trying to eat. Or if they do, then there's more than enough niche websites to cater for them.

6. It can make less well-endowed or anorexic women feel uncomfortable about their bodies and they might go on to have serious body-image issues.

7. Similarly, it can make women who can't breastfeed feel inferior and plunge them into an ever-deeper post-natal depression from which they might never recover.

8. The sight of an exposed breast can quite easily turn a man's head, overwhelm him with desire and break up a marriage. One of my UKIP colleagues saw a woman nursing her baby on a train and left his wife that evening.

9. It can also cause men to become infatuated and lose focus. One of our funders was a chief executive of a successful FTSE 100 company. He saw a breastfeeding mother in a hotel lobby and became obsessed with nipples to such an effect that his job suffered. He lost a shareholder vote of confidence and now sells bunches of flowers at traffic lights.

10. Just because it's natural doesn't make it right. Sex, urination and defecation are all natural but you wouldn't do those in the middle of Starbucks. I hope.

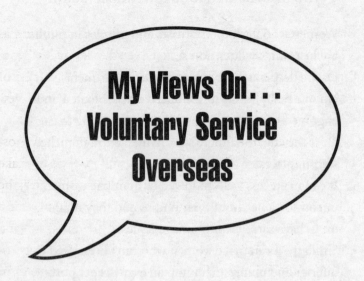

My Views On...
Voluntary Service
Overseas

There are some things to feel quite ashamed about, like once being a fan of Gordon Brown or stealing the Hospice Charity Box from the counter at McDonalds – but 'colonial guilt' is definitely not one of them.

Why would anyone ever give up their God-given freedom of choice and put themselves at the mercy of some smarmy ex-Foreign Office do-gooder who'll stick a pin in a map of Africa, Asia or the Indian sub-continent and send you to some godforsaken country where you'll need a course of injections just to stop you dying when you set foot across its border? And if you do survive hepatitis, beri-beri or Ebola and a monsoon season that lasts from January to December you'll find yourself doing a job that's far worse than the worst student holiday job you've ever had, even if that job was artificially inseminating turkeys or working as a quality controller in a ball bearing factory. Let me tell you, digging latrines in Namibia or teaching English to a tribe of headhunters in a scorpion-infested grass hut in Papua New Guinea is no picnic.

We're taught nowadays that Great Britain exploited most of the population of its former Empire and it's time to make restitution. Well, consider this… The countries to which the VSO send you will be lacking in three things: a) running water, b) electricity and c) the concept of a fair day's pay for a fair day's work. Yes. That's right. Not only are you expected to put up with conditions that would even have contestants in *I'm A Celebrity* walking out in disgust but you don't even get paid for your time.

Now who's being exploited?

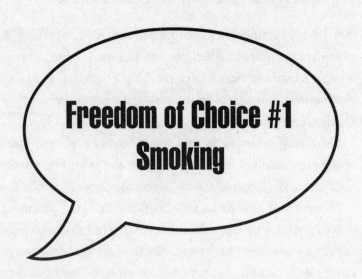

Freedom of Choice #1
Smoking

Just as standing in queues and not reeking of garlic differentiates the British from foreigners, freedom of choice is what differentiates democracies from dictatorships.

This is a cornerstone of UKIP beliefs (the bit about freedom of choice, not the queuing or the reeking of garlic thing – although those are very important too). As a party we firmly believe that the individual should be free to do whatever he or she wants as long as this does not limit the freedom of choice of another individual in society.*

This principle applies to a number of issues which we'll address throughout this book, starting with a freedom I hold particularly dear, and which is under severe threat from our so-called EU masters: the freedom to smoke.

*Unless of course you're part of a minority group because another cornerstone of our beliefs is that the needs of the many outweigh the needs of the few.

25 Reasons Why It's Good to Smoke

1. Buying cigarettes from corner shops helps support local businesses.
2. Buying cigarettes from anywhere helps fund new hospitals and schools.
3. You'll always have something to do with your hands.
4. If you don't smoke it looks like you can't afford cigarettes.
5. If you work with dynamite or fireworks, you'll always have a convenient method of lighting the fuse.
6. Having to stand outside your place of employment helps to break up the working day.
7. Having to stand outside a bar or restaurant is a great way to meet people.
8. That ingrained smell on your coat makes it easy to pick it out of a pile at a party.
9. It gives you a genuine excuse for loitering: 'Sorry officer, I was just finishing my cigarette.'
10. You'll have a real reason to repaint the ceilings.
11. Although I'm not condoning it, you can accept benefits from the government without guilt, knowing you've paid more in taxes.
12. You'll keep your weight down.

13. You can amuse young children (and impressionable members of the opposite sex) by blowing smoke rings.
14. If you like feeling unwell it feeds your need for attention.
15. Accidentally burning holes in your clothes gives you a reason to keep updating your wardrobe and keep with the current trends.
16. Your ex-partner always wanted you to stop and you don't want to give him/her the satisfaction.
17. Yellow fingers and teeth really coordinate with blonde hair.
18. It dulls your sense of smell so you can't be tempted by the delicious aroma of fatty food.
19. Occasional house fires help keep the fire brigade on their toes.
20. Giving up would make you ratty and irritable… why inflict that on your friends?
21. A husky voice is very sexy.
22. That hacking cough and phlegm makes you realise you're still alive.
23. That ashen expression and extra wrinkles around your mouth give you that 'mature' look.
24. It keeps tobacco factory workers in employment.
25. Ditto cancer specialists.

My Views On...
Fairtrade

Whatever happened to market forces and the laws of supply and demand? Have we suddenly abandoned these bedrocks of the economy? And why aren't we giving British growers of cocoa, bananas or coffee financial assistance?

By subsidising Fairtrade farmers in developing countries we're sending out a message that it's okay to be inefficient, that competition is unfair and that 'yes', in these times of an uncertain economy and the need for fiscal prudence, it's quite acceptable for us to pay a 20p premium for a grande skinny cinnamon dolce mocha Frappuccino. Is that what we really want?

And just look at the Fairtrade products supermarkets are foisting on us. They're all basically like Lidl versions of the real products we love, but with an odd taste. Take chocolate for example. Supporters of Fairtrade say it's more than just chocolate; it's hope in a bar. No it's not. It's laxative in a bar. Something made with 80 per cent cocoa can only give you two things: a bitter taste and the squits. And then there's Fairtrade wine. Apparently we drink over 10 million litres of Fairtrade wine in the UK each year. I say 'we' because I've only drunk half a mouthful before spitting it out like mouthwash… which it bore more than a passing resemblance to. Chile is better known for producing military dictatorships than fine wines and I once tried a Pinot Grigio produced by a cooperative vineyard in the Huasco Valley. The label said the wine had a 'perky' favour; it was half right. It should have said Pinky and Perky because it tasted like pork.

Those misguided fools who support Fairtrade say they're quite happy to pay extra in order to fund social developmental projects on plantations. Well I don't know about you, but I'm finding it hard enough to pay for my own kids' education, let alone fund some dump of a junior school in Guatemala.

Great Britons No. 1
William Shakespeare

Playwright, poet, actor and all-round decent bloke!
As far as I'm concerned, Shakespeare is the world's pre-eminent dramatist but don't just take my word for it, even Wikipedia agrees. He grew up in middle England in Stratford-upon-Avon, a charming English Cotswolds town with some really nice, traditional pubs, and he was a self-made man. Despite not having an Eton education or a privileged upbringing, not only did he rise to be one of the greatest playwrights in the world but he married an A-list actress too. As they say, the boy done good!

Shakespeare's plays are performed more often than those of any other playwright in the world including Tim Rice, and that's quite an achievement. And don't even bother comparing him to some of your foreign playwrights; there's no contest! Take Molière for instance. He's meant to be one of the greatest masters of comedy (not my words, God no) but have you seen *The Misanthrope* or *The Imaginary Invalid*? Mr Bean or Benny Hill would knock both of these into a cocked hat. What's more, Molière only wrote 31 plays compared to Shakespeare's 38: another example of your typical Gallic lethargy.

Like UKIP, Shakespeare was very broadminded in his outlook on life. He was just as happy writing about those from Bongo Bongo land (*Othello*), the gays (Antonio from *Twelfth Night*), the Jews (Shylock) and cripples (*Richard III*), as he was writing about normal people, and that's to be highly commended. Apart from being prolific he could turn his hand to anything... historical plays, tragedies, comedies – even tragi-comedies, whatever they are – and whatever he wrote was good and there were no cheesy songs like 'Any Dream Will Do' or 'Don't Cry for Me Argentina'. What's more, at that time women weren't allowed to act, so that meant that when you visited the Globe Theatre you didn't have to suffer the Elizabethan equivalent of Elaine Paige.

Shakespeare is also recognised for giving the English language upwards of 1,700 new words, including 'zany', 'madcap' and 'scuffle'. But what's even better is that he also came up with some great insults, such as this one from *As You Like It*: 'Thou art like a toad; ugly and venomous.'

It's as if he actually knew Angela Merkel.

Will. Shakespeare   1622

Charity Begins at Home

These days you can't walk down the high street without going past retail outlets that resemble more of an explosion at a jumble sale than anything that looks remotely like offering an appealing shopping experience. These are charity shops.

Now don't get me wrong. I'm not against charity shops per se. Anything that supports the fight against terrible ailments and diseases or helps old folk is laudable. The fact that our town centres are blighted with so many of them is a damning indictment against Coalition cutbacks in health care and clinical research.

What I do have a problem with, however, is charity shops where the money collected goes overseas. Why on earth would you want to do that? A pound given to the Romanian orphans is a pound less for the Spastics. And anyway, their parents should be taking care of them – not UK taxpayers.

But what gets my goat more than anything is Oxfam charity shops where the money goes to the third world. Or as they call it, 'developing countries'. And as a side note, most of these so-called developing countries are in sub-Saharan Africa, which have had civilisations dating back to 2500BC… Bloody hell! How many years does it take for a country to develop?

Anyway, I digress. My other problem is that there's absolutely no way of telling if the money will actually reach the so-called needy people in these countries. Ask a member of staff for a written assurance that any money you spend will actually go to the poor and not end up in the pocket of some third-world despot who'll spend it all on AK-47 machine guns, gold-plated taps for his palace en suite or a new top-of-the-range convertible Bentley, and you'll get a puzzled look from someone scratching their beard. And that's just the women.

So, for those who think like me, I've produced this handy guide so you can recognise an Oxfam shop and walk straight past it.

How to Recognise an Oxfam Shop*

There are three basic clues:
1. Window displays that reveal a level of flair and attractiveness some way between 99p shops and shoe-repair kiosks.

2. Staff so worthy and self-righteous that they make Jesus look like a degenerate.
3. A range of merchandise absolutely no one wants. Where else, apart from skips or bonfires, would you find the following?:

- Whitesnake, Alison Moyet and Dexy's Midnight Runners LPs
- VHS copies of *The Fly II*, *Top Gun* and anything featuring Rosanna Arquette
- Ties so wide and gaudy that even Nelson Mandela wouldn't wear one
- Joanna Lumley and Sir Alex Ferguson autobiographies
- Disappointing paperbacks by Jilly Cooper, Jackie Collins and Harold Robbins
- Ten-year-old cricketing yearbooks
- Jigsaws with at least 15 per cent of the pieces missing
- A range of ethnic handicrafts that redefine the words 'unnecessary' and 'ugly'
- Bars of chocolate with levels of cocoa concentrate so high that you will likely get diarrhoea just by smelling them. Or reading the label
- A small wooden car made by someone who has never, ever seen a car in their life and probably never will
- Clothing that still smells of dead people

*Apart from the fact that it will say Oxfam in big letters on its fascia. But that's just detail.

The UKIP Anthem

We had the 'UKIP Calypso' out last year as a sort of unofficial theme song and it was really funny. And poignant, of course, but I got a lot of flak because it was sung in a fake Caribbean accent. Bloody hellfire! It's a calypso isn't it? How else is it meant to be sung? With a Brummie twang or a South African… well, whatever you call that abominable accent of theirs? Anyway, that's water under the bridge, so for this year I decided to take a less controversial route and instead write an anthem based on the worldwide hit 'YMCA' by the Village People. Okay, they might not be the sort of people we want in our country, I mean party, and they're probably all married to each other by now, but it's a really catchy ditty. Enjoy.

U.K.I.P.

(to be sung to the tune of 'YMCA')

Young man, if you hate the EU
I said, young man, I want you in my crew
I said, young man, spread the word that it's true
There's no need to be in Europe

It costs, fifty million a day
I said, young man, that's a huge price to pay
Jean-Claude Juncker, is so surly and rude
Which leads all of us to conclude

It's good to vote for the U.K.I.P.
It's good to vote for the U.K.I.P.

We have policies, designed to incite
You can hang out towards the right

It's good to vote for the U.K.I.P.
It's good to vote for the U.K.I.P.

You can get yourself heard; you can protect your job
You can even join a lynch mob

Young man, this country's a mess
I said, young man, look at the NHS

I said, young man, you really don't have to guess
The immigrants, it must be their fault

At the, borders there's a long queue
I said, Poles and the Romanians too
Here to plumb and build, or put up a shelf
If you were arsed, you'd do it yourself

It's good to vote for the U.K.I.P.
It's good to vote for the U.K.I.P.

We have policies, designed to incite
You can hang out towards the right

It's good to vote for the U.K.I.P.
It's good to vote for the U.K.I.P.

You can get yourself heard; you can protect your job
You can even join a lynch mob

Young man, I was once in your shoes
I said, I was down and out with the blues
I felt hardship, I felt adversity
A victim, of diversity

That's when someone came up to me,
And said, young man, there's something you ought to see
It's a party, awash in purple and yellow

A great bunch of decent fellows

It's good to vote for the U.K.I.P.
It's good to vote for the U.K.I.P.

We have policies, designed to incite
You can hang out towards the right

U.K.I.P. It's good to vote for the U.K.I.P.

Young man, young man; there's no need to feel shame
Young man, young man; you know who's to blame

U.K.I.P. It's good to vote for the U.K.I.P.

Young man, young man; there's no need to feel shame
Young man, young man; you know who's to blame

U.K.I.P. It's good to vote for the U.K.I.P.
[to fade]

Why Don't the Chattering Classes Just Shut Their Gobs?

Sometime I feel like I'm Hitler. And when I say that, I mean from a Second World War strategic point of view, of course.

What I'm alluding to is that I'm having to use the limited resources at my disposal to fight simultaneously on two fronts. In his case it was the Red Army to the east and the advancing allies to the west. In my case I'm battling not just against the bully boys of the EU but those within my own country who are trying to defeat me. I'm talking about the so-called liberal elite (their words, not mine), the Chattering Classes.*

You know the sort of people I mean… the type that drink Fairtrade coffee, re-use hessian shopping bags, host Oscar parties and make sure they offset their carbon footprint (which doesn't need offsetting as global warming is an obvious lie, but that's another issue anyway).

I know it's wrong to generalise and stereotype, like saying that all French people are arrogant, all Bulgarians are lazy and all Nigerians are scam artists – but most stereotypes persist because they are actually based on fact. Such it is with the Chattering Classes…

The UKIP Guide to Identifying a Member of the Chattering Classes

They don't have a TV

It's not because they think that most programmes appeal to the lowest common denominator or because they abhor the political bias of the BBC. The only reason they don't have a TV is purely so they can tell other people they don't have a TV.

They eat in fusion restaurants

Forget Chinese, Indian, Italian – even Lebanese, Vietnamese and Cuban… they're all 'so last year' as far as the Chattering Classes are concerned. That's why you'll see them tucking into some Frankenstein abomination in über trendy restaurants that combine, for example, Hungarian and Nigerian, Lebanese and Icelandic, or Australian and Scandinavian cuisine… Salted ostrich and herring pie anyone?

They have lots of kitchen gadgets

Apart from the homeware department of John Lewis, where else can you see the following gadgets but in the kitchen of a member of the Chattering Classes: electric garlic press, ravioli crimper, individual egg cooker, pineapple core remover, pasta maker and avocado de-stoner. And do you absolutely, positively have to have six rice steamers to cater for white, brown, black, long grain, basmati and pilau?

They drive a Toyota Prius

Although described as a car for those who know nothing about cars and even less about real world fuel economy, the Prius does come with a lot of features as standard. These include extra self-satisfaction, an abundance of righteousness and added smugness. There are cheaper, cleaner and more economical cars than the Prius but the Chattering Classes don't care. They buy them in droves not because they're better for the environment, but because they make a statement. And that statement is: 'I'm a prick'.

Their pushchairs have three wheels

The only reason for a buggy to have a large sticky-out wheel at the front is so you can whack it into other peoples' shins and ankles and make them even more aware that you're a Chattering Classes parent. Oversize and shod with knobbly tyres that look like you could transport your child to safety from the bottom of a deep quarry, these impractical pushchairs are new mothers' first priority after bringing a new life into the world. That, and enrolling their newborn in baby yoga classes.

They eat cheese no one has ever heard of

Wine bores at Chattering Classes dinner parties have been replaced by cheese bores. These are people who know their Lüneberg from their Limburger and their Harbourne Blue from their Bleu d'Auvergne – and won't let you forget. Naturally, they buy their cheeses from either a specialist gourmet store or the local farmers market and will say things like, 'Of course, you realise that it's the addition of cream to the whey that differentiates a manouri from a feta.' Or, 'You'll just love this remarkable bryndza from the Ukraine. It's crumbly yet slightly moist with a characteristic tang, evocative of the savoury Liptauer from Vienna.'

But you already knew that.

Their children are all gifted

Irrespective of their child's ability or performance at school (usually a Free School founded by Toby Young), all Chattering Classes parents claim their little Lucien or Jocasta is gifted. If their child is an academic over-achiever then the accolade naturally applies. If they're disruptive or suffer from ADHD then this is because they're too bright for school and get awfully frustrated; and if their child is as thick as two short planks, it's because they're far too creative or far too advanced to care about the minutiae of lessons. It's a win-win-win situation.

*So called because they just like to hear themselves talk.

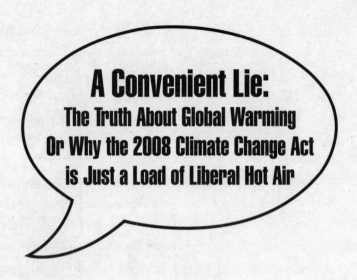

A Convenient Lie:
The Truth About Global Warming
Or Why the 2008 Climate Change Act
is Just a Load of Liberal Hot Air

First they called it global warming but when they noticed that some parts of the world were experiencing severe freezes they renamed it, conveniently, climate change.

And by 'they' I mean environmentalists.

And by 'environmentalists' I mean crackpot liars.

How can you take these people seriously when they can't even agree on the so-called apocalyptic consequences of climate change? Some say the polar ice caps will melt, flooding coastal areas and submerging whole island nations like Atlantis. Others say the build-up of greenhouse gases will make the earth the same temperature as Venus, evaporating every single last drop of water on the planet. And I say, it's not going to happen.

Sure, the temperature of the earth rises and falls and the

weather changes just like… well, like the weather – but it's always done that. Here are two words that might give you a clue as to why: the Sun. So how do I know it's a purely natural phenomenon? Well, I'm not going to get all sciencey and bamboozle you with boring statistics about CO_2 levels, ozone depletion, glacial retreat or Arctic sea ice loss. That's detail and as you know, I'm a Big Picture Man.

And for me, the Big Picture is that it's all a scam perpetuated by desperate, grasping scientists trying to make a name for themselves and get their hands on huge research grants. Sadly, those gullible idiots in the Labour Party and at the EU fell for it hook, line and sinker and they set targets for reducing CO_2 emissions. The result is that the EU is now making us buy those stupid twisty energy-saving light bulbs that have to warm up like an old TV set and give as much illumination as a baby's night light, and vacuum cleaners that suck as much as Vince Cable's business skills.

Plus, under the guise of 'reduced emissions' they foist rubbish small engine Citroën, Renault and Peugeot hatch-backs on to us – not to help the environment but to help the French car industry.

But the worst offender of all the politicians is Al Gore who, in 2006, wrote *An Inconvenient Truth*. In this he called the threat of global warming 'the most serious problem our civilization faces'.

He's wrong.

It's lying politicians.

8 Reasons I Know Global Warming Is a Lie

1. If the earth were really getting warmer it would cost less to heat our homes. Have you taken a look at your fuel bills lately?

2. Warmer temperatures would also mean that we get fewer colds. I don't know about you but my Lemsip expenditure has remained static.

3. By now, if you believe all the CO_2 data, the greenhouse effect should have turned Africa into a lush wilderness. Really? I recently looked at photos of the Sudan and photos taken by NASA's Mars Rover… and I couldn't tell the difference.

4. If it were hotter you'd expect a run on Factor 4 sun cream at Boots. I went into my local branch and they had plenty of bottles. Not just that, but loads of after sun too.

5. Likewise, I've been extremely worried that my local newsagent would run out of Strawberry Mivvis and Magnums, but the ice cream freezer at Mr Patel's is always full (albeit exorbitantly expensive).

6. Increased CO_2 would act like a fertilizer. Add the fact that warmer weather would lead to longer growing seasons and higher food production and, as a consequence, lower prices… So how come I went into my local Morrisons last Wednesday and prices were as expensive as Mr Patel's?

7. Warmer temperatures would mean there'd be no need for a winter wardrobe. Some hope! Last December my wife

still went out and bought a pair of brand new high wedge-heel calf boots and a quilted long zip coat. Women!

8. Why hasn't Blackpool become the equivalent of Monte Carlo or Cannes? Last time I visited they still had bingo halls instead of casinos and donkeys instead of super yachts (though the locals did have a strange accent, I'll give you that).

Citizenship Test

The Government calls it a way of checking that immigrants have a satisfactory knowledge of British life and adequate knowledge of English. I call it a bad pub quiz... and I've seen enough of those.

The main problem is that the current test, introduced by Labour, is completely irrelevant and also far too easy. Who cares when women were allowed the vote* or how old Big Ben is? And you've got to be incredibly stupid not to know the country where Welsh is spoken or the name of the bloke who built Hadrian's Wall. Yes... these are actual questions.

When UKIP gets into power we're going to scrap the current online 'Life in the UK' Test and replace it with one that's far more appropriate to people wanting to settle here. And by more appropriate, I mean making sure we only accept the right type of people. At the end of the day you can't give citizenship away like some cheap free gift you get with a Happy Meal.

*In my view, 'why' would be a better question than 'when', but that's another matter.

The UKIP Life in the UK Test

Time allowed: 20 minutes

Rules
1. Answer all the questions by clicking the appropriate statement. That's it. Even a foreigner should be able to cope with that.
2. If you score over 100 points you will be allowed to remain in the country.
For now.

NB. This is the only version of the test. There isn't one where we've wasted good money translating it into your native language, not even if your native language isn't really a language at all, but more a collection of random doodles that look more like Klingon than a proper alphabet.

WARNING

You have to complete this test yourself. There's no point getting one of your extended family to take it for you and think just because you're swarthy and look alike, we won't find out… we will. We can do this as we have a very particular set of skills. Skills that make UKIP a nightmare for people like you. If you complete the test properly, that will be the end of it. We will not look for you, we will not pursue you. But if you don't, we will look for you, we will find you, and we will kill you.

SECTION 1
QUESTIONS ABOUT YOURSELF

Using the following paint shades, how would you describe the colour of your skin?

- Cool white   [10 points]
- Ivory   [8 points]
- White with a hint of brown   [4 points]
- Buttercup yellow   [2 points]
- Deep vanilla   [2 points]
- Sweet caramel   [2 points]
- Rich walnut   [2 points]
- Coffee kiss   [2 points]
- Evening shadow   [2 points]

- Midnight charcoal   [2 points]
- Deep ebony   [2 points]

Ethnically speaking, which of these Walt Disney films do you most feel an affinity with?

- *Mary Poppins*   [5 points]
- *Snow White*   [4 points]
- *The Hunchback of Notre Dame*   [3 points]
- *Mulan*   [2 points]
- *Pocahontas*   [2 points]
- *Aladdin*   [1 point]
- *The Lion King*   [1 point]
- *The Little Mermaid*   [0 points]

Can you say 'The rain in Spain stays mainly in the plain' just like Professor Higgins in *My Fair Lady*?

- Cor blimey! I'll 'ave a go guv!   [5 points]
- But of course   [3 points]
- Professor who?   [0 points]

If you achieve residency what would you bring to this country?

- Professional skills and a meaningful
  contribution to the social fabric   [5 points]
- Additional tax revenue and a positive
  impact on economic growth   [4 points]

- Someone's who's happy to be part of the underclass, who knows their place in society, who is happy to do shitty jobs and not claim benefits   [3 points]
- A birth rate more associated with cats and dogs than humans   [0 points]
- All my family   [0 points]
- An archaic seventh-century world view and a bloodbath   [0 points]
- Ebola   [0 points]

SECTION 2
QUESTIONS ABOUT THE COUNTRY
OF YOUR BIRTH

What is its Gross National Product measured in?
- Thousands of billions of dollars   [5 points]
- Hundreds of billions of dollars   [4 points]
- Millions of dollars   [1 point]
- Coconuts   [0 points]

What are its main exports?
- Machinery/electronic equipment   [10 points]
- Vehicles   [10 points]
- Pharmaceutical products   [10 points]
- Iron and steel   [8 points]

- Oil [3 points]
- Mangos [2 points]
- Asylum seekers [2 points]
- Malaria [1 point]
- Internet scams [1 point]
- Refugees [1 point]
- Suicide bombers [0 points]

Does your country's national costume include any of the following?

- We're quite normal and don't have a national costume [10 points]
- Something that involves an apron or knee length trousers [7 points]
- Leather shorts [5 points]
- Anything involving copious amounts of lace [4 points]
- Poncho [4 points]
- Embroidered gypsy blouson [3 points]
- Colourful tribal fabrics [2 points]
- A length of bright cloth that just wraps round you. That's it. [2 points]
- Pointy shoes that roll up at the end [1 point]
- Tartan [0 points]

What do the letters in your alphabet look like?
- The same as the letters in this test [5 points]
- Nearly the same as the letters in this
  test but also including a back-to-front R,
  something that looks like the symbol for
  pi and a few other funny things [2 points]
- Lots of squiggly shapes and symbols [1 point]

How do you write?
- Left to right [5 points]
- Right to left [2 points]
- Up to down [2 points]
- I can't write [0 points]

SECTION 3
QUESTIONS ABOUT YOUR RELIGION

Does your God have a son called Jesus?
- Yes [10 points]
- No [0 points]

When is your version of Christmas?
- On 25 December of course [10 points]
- It all depends on the moon [0 points]

SECTION 4
QUESTIONS ABOUT BRITISH
CULTURE AND CUSTOMS

Which of these classic comedy catchphrases do you find the funniest?

- 'Listen. I will say zis only once'   [5 points]
- 'Good Moaning'   [5 points]
- 'You stupid boy!'   [3 points]
- 'I'm free!'   [1 point]
- 'I'm the only gay in the village'   [0 points]

How would you prepare a nice cup of tea?

- Milk goes in first   [5 points]
- Tea goes in first   [5 points]
- I drink herbal tea so I don't need milk   [3 points]
- What's tea? Where I come from we have
  a traditional aniseed-flavoured drink that
  we sip seated near our camels   [1 point]

What food are you most likely to enjoy for Sunday lunch?

- Roast beef, Yorkshire puds, roast potatoes
  and all the trimmings   [5 points]
- Kangaroo penis and wichetty grub   [3 points]
- Jerk chicken and deep-fried slices of yam   [1 point]

- Mutabbag Bel Laham and Tabbouleh   [1 point]
- The country I come from is so poor we
  don't have the concept of lunch. Or food. [0 points]

Why would you go to a British pub?
- To meet like-minded individuals and
  have an ill-informed discussion about
  immigration   [5 points]
- To sample the best ales in the known
  world   [4 points]
- It's a great opportunity to meet other
  people and start a fight   [2 points]
- An indefinable soul or spirit that just
  makes you feel at home   [2 points]

In your view, which of these defines the concept of Britishness? (you may choose more than one)
- A strongly-held belief that some cultures
  are intrinsically superior to others   [5 points]
- Fair play, free speech and obesity   [4 points]
- Bad food, a useless national football
  team, intolerance   [3 points]

10 Things That Really Wind Me Up About Eastern Europe

Some people reading this section might say, 'Nigel, it's wrong to generalise. How can you lump every single Eastern European country under one heading?' Well, until someone can explain to me the main differences between Latvia and Lithuania, Slovakia and Slovenia, or Bosnia and Herzegovina, I'll happily continue thinking of them all as some sort of gelatinous whole. In my capacity as an MEP I've had to suffer many fact-finding visits to these countries, all of which are still finding it difficult to wrench themselves away from over forty-five years of Soviet rule. Frankly, once you've been to one place which offers concrete tower blocks that redefine the words brutal and repugnant, as well as widespread official corruption and toxic levels of air pollution, you've been to them all.

1. Hospitality can change into hostility at a moment's notice

One moment you might be enjoying a beer with the locals in a friendly bar; the next you might be smashed in the face by a broken glass. All it takes is for you to casually mention something complimentary about a neighbouring country or its people, unaware that the only reason the other country exists is because of a brutal bloody civil war (usually involving a massacre) that split the nation in two. As a guide, no matter where you are, it's best not to mention any of the states of the former Yugoslavia.

Particularly Serbia.

2. You're surrounded by old people with miserable, staring eyes

They're everywhere in Eastern Europe. In the street and shops. On the trains, trams and buses. Their expression is one of resentment, jealousy, bitterness and unbridled hatred. You'll find that most of them work in the hospitality and service industries.

3. Taxi drivers that settle discussions over fares with knives

An abundance of unscrupulous taxi drivers charge fares based more on a whim than a meter and will often add a range of compulsory 'extras' when you arrive at your destination. Taking rides in these cabs will leave you ripped off and/or ripped open.

4. There's always someone willing to pick a fight with you
Rampant alcoholism and cultures that equate heavy drinking with machismo means it's very easy for visitors to get into trouble in Eastern Europe. In order to stay out of trouble it's best to have a basic knowledge of the local language and mixed martial arts.

5. You'll be bothered by a beggar every 100 paces
Travelling around Eastern Europe is like being in a place where 60 per cent of the country's population are *Big Issue* sellers who are handy with a knife.

6. Two-tier pricing
When ordering drinks expect to be charged at least three or four times what the locals pay. Don't cause a scene with the barman unless you feel like discussing this inequality with a burly member of the Russian Mafia, who has a vested interest in most bars and clubs east of Prague.

7. 1960s standards of technology
Ask if a café has wifi and you'll be laughed at; either that or you'll be burned as a witch.

8. There's no understanding of the term 'personal space'
East Europeans feel most comfortable talking to you a nose length from your face, or queuing so closely behind you that they are virtually committing a sex act.

9. Public transport timings are given with the same degree of accuracy as reading tea leaves

It doesn't matter what you're told in a hotel, train or bus station, travel agent or government office, the timetables of East European public transport services are compiled with an accuracy of plus or minus 16 hours. Dealing tarot, throwing rune stones or examining animal entrails will provide you with a greater degree of precision.

10. Old men carrying goats and chickens on modern trains and buses

The guidebooks will say this is charming or quaint. To everyone else it's noisy and unhygienic.

My Views On...
Corporal Punishment in School

Punishment as a consequence of wrongdoing has a long history in Britain and with good reason. Just take two examples; if Charles I hadn't been beheaded or if Dick Turpin hadn't been hanged, then what we'd be doing is telling society that treason is acceptable; that robbing people with pistols is fine. Children have to learn at an early age to take responsibility for bad behaviour and by 'at an early age', I mean as soon as they can make the connection between their conduct and pain.

When I was at school, being smacked was a way of life, as it was for many of my contemporaries (although at Eton they called it spanking). It didn't do us any harm and a lot of the Eton boys actually liked it; just ask David Cameron. Anyway, I digress. Children today are far more unruly and disrespectful in the classroom and need to be taught right from wrong. Role models like Miley Cyrus, Justin Bieber and Simon Cowell make them think it's OK to be rude, selfish, irritating and evil.

Critics say that corporal punishment doesn't work. Really? Well, before corporal punishment in the classroom was abolished there were no school shootings and very few examples of gruesome beheadings by religious nutcases.

At the end of the day all I'm talking about is a series of short, sharp smacks with a non-flexible object. Because I believe in freedom the number of strikes and the type of object used (e.g. cane, paddle, big shoe, cricket bat, etc.) will be down to individual schools.

Critics say that smacking kids can cause psychological problems in later life but look at the alternatives to smacking… hitting them with a sock filled with coins, punching them in the face, kicking them… Is this what the do-gooders want? Is it? If they do then just bear in mind it's a short move from this to waterboarding.

Let me just leave you with two thoughts on the matter. Actions speak louder than words, and Kim Jong-un wasn't smacked as a child…

My Guide to Countries That Don't Count

Moldova, Azerbaijan, Montenegro, Belarus.
Really?

These places might as well be totally fictitious states like Ruritania or Freedonia; hardly anyone would know the difference and even fewer would care.

These and a few more nations like them are what we call 'courtesy countries', founded after ethnic strife or civil wars, just to appease whining citizens who were constantly bleating on about independence.

To be honest, these places don't really count for anything and are basically just irritating pimples on the spotty backside of the European mainland. They're countries more closely associated with civil unrest, poverty and communism than with top travel destinations.

The biggest issue though is that it won't be too long before they're invited to join the EU. When that happens not only will they be given huge bailouts by the European Central Bank but we'll have thousands of Moldovans or Montenegroes turning up uninvited on our shores. And if that's not bad enough, another repercussion will be yet more ethnically-derived soft rock in the Eurovision Song Contest.

Consider the following less of a travel guide and more of a warning...

Moldova

A former Soviet Republic, sandwiched between Romania and the Ukraine, Moldova is a hilly country that slopes towards two things. One is the Black Sea and the other is economic meltdown. As one of the poorest countries in Europe, with a huge foreign debt and massive unemployment, Moldova is still heavily dependent on Russia. However, two thirds of Moldovans are of Romanian descent and the country is immensely proud of its Romanian roots. By this I presume they mean hordes of children begging at train stations and a thriving black-market economy.

Anyway, Moldova is famous for its wealth of traditional folk art; so if carpet-making, pottery and weaving float your boat, you'll have a ball here. Other things guaranteed to prolong your stay include a 600-year-old oak tree and 30 monasteries and wooden churches. Surprisingly, Moldova is also very famous for its wines and is among the world's top wine exporters. As you know I'm a bit of a wine buff and I'd say that while some Moldovan reds can be compared to the best Angolan whites, most can be identified by a number of common characteristics; a bouquet of burning tyres, the flavour of pine-scented Toilet Duck and the aftertaste of cough linctus.

Capital city: Chişinău

Moldovans describe their capital as a great party city. This is probably correct if your idea of a great party involves bad wine (see above) and music that hasn't been heard since the Rubettes and Mud graced the charts. Entry into Chişinău is via the Holy Gates, Moldova's answer to the Arc de Triomphe (though there's absolutely nothing to be triumphant about). Proof of the city's aspirations to embrace western ideals is the fact that there's a KFC and a two-storey McDonalds.

Azerbaijan

Another former Soviet Republic, Azerbaijan is located at the crossroads of Eastern Europe and Western Asia and is said to offer visitors the 'very best of both worlds'.

Don't be fooled though. Just as there are no best parts of being kicked in the balls, there are no best parts of Eastern Europe or Western Asia – unless you're a fan of an oppressive political regime, rampant corruption, hundreds of thousands of refugees and a culture embedded in superstition.

Unlike many of its counterparts in the region, Azerbaijan

is a relatively prosperous country with significant western investment in its vast oil fields and natural gas reserves. Despite this wealth from oil exports, visitors here will still feel short changed. Tourist attractions range from the predictable to the dreary and include tangerine groves, a men-only public bath, the remains of a demolished castle and 400 mud volcanoes (although in my book, if you've seen one mud volcano you've seen them all). In winter you can ski from the Shahdag Mountain Resort, known within Azerbaijan as the 'playground of the rich'. However it's important to point out that this description is relative in a country where, for many people, instant coffee and shoes are considered luxury goods.

Capital city: Baku

The old Inner City area is described as beguiling, but an abundance of narrow streets and alleyways is enticing only if you're a pickpocket. The newer downtown area is where you'll find the hotels and tourist attractions including the world's third tallest flagpole and the Flame Towers, which sounds exciting but it's just a skyscraper housing offices and apartments. There's also the State Carpet Museum where for about £15 you can wear a traditional Azerbaijan costume and have your photo taken against a backdrop of carpets. Whoopee shit.

MONTENEGRO

Being surrounded by Albania, Serbia, Croatia, Kosovo, and Bosnia & Herzegovina meant that travel to Montenegro in the 1990s used to be a minefield. Literally. The Yugoslav wars decimated the tourist industry and it's only since its independence from Serbia in 2006 that Montenegro has managed to regain its reputation as *the* place to visit if every other southern European resort is fully booked. What it lacks in style and sophistication it more than makes up for with uncomfortably hot summer temperatures, overcrowded beaches, ubiquitous loud Eurobeat music, countless stalls selling knock-off Louis Vuitton, and simmering resentment between the two states.

Promoting its beaches, mountains and night life, the government of Montenegro is committed to making its country an 'elite tourist destination' and in 2010 Yahoo! Travel listed Montenegro as one of the 10 Top Hot Spots to visit, although I assume this was a typo. The tourist board claim that the country's reputation as a truly fashionable destination was sealed in *Casino Royale* when Daniel Craig's James Bond played a high-stakes poker tournament at Montenegro's Hotel Splendid. What they forget to point out is that the filmmakers decided to shoot the whole scene in the Czech Republic.

Those flying into the country's two international airports should be reassured that they'll be reunited with their luggage within 72 hours.

Capital city: Podgorica

Characterised by brutal Communist-era architecture, Podgorica pays homage to a glut of ugly fortress-like concrete structures and creates an impression of a sterile, dismal, cold, depressing hell-hole... it's difficult to think of a more perfect place to commit suicide. However, for those who do decide to carry on living, the city's stunning attractions include a monument to honour the famous Russian poet, writer, theatre and film actor, Vladimir Vysotsky, plus a puppet theatre and a nightclub called Mr Cool.

BELARUS

Visitors here tend to fall into three categories: people retracing their roots, human rights workers and those who have got lost. Of course, if you don't fall into any of these groups there's nothing to stop you enjoying a trip to Belarus, apart from overwhelming boredom and a high probability of getting picked up by the secret police. Although Belarus achieved independence from the Soviet Union in 1991 there's still an air of despondency throughout the country, fuelled by the legacy of massacres and purges by both the Red Army and the Nazis, and more recently, by a failing economy and a tyrannical, authoritarian regime.

There's also the aftermath of Chernobyl in neighbouring Ukraine; after the 1986 disaster 25 per cent of what is now Belarus was exposed to significant radiation. So, if a repressive government and nuclear contamination don't put you off, a trip here offers many things for the intrepid traveller including a cuisine that assimilates a mix of influences from surrounding countries. However, you need to bear in mind that Belarus's neighbours are Russia, Ukraine, Poland, Lithuania and Latvia – countries that are far better at manufacturing tractors than they are at creating fine food.

Capital city: Minsk

If you really want to experience what Moscow was like in the Cold War, visit Minsk. Rebuilt after being obliterated in the Second World War, the best that can be said about the architecture is that the buildings are foreboding and grim. Wide empty streets teem with a constant police and military presence while obedient locals go about their business with a fear that their every move is being monitored. It is.

Telecommunications are stuck in the 1960s and most attractions are closed, suspended or under reconstruction. Lee Harvey Oswald lived in Minsk for a while. No wonder he shot Kennedy.

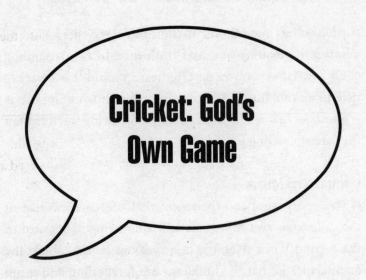

Cricket: God's Own Game

'I don't like cricket, I love it.'

Every time I hear 10cc's 'Dreadlock Holiday' I find myself singing along, nodding in agreement and saying, 'Yeah mon'. People criticised the 'UKIP Calypso' when it came out, but if you listen to the 10cc song you can see that Mike Read's Caribbean accent is really authentic. But why do I and so many UKIP members love cricket?

Well, it's civilised and civilising. When we conquered lots of the countries in Bongo Bongo land we introduced cricket and slavery and it's good to see at least one of them is still popular. In some of these countries cricket is almost seen as a religion, and even here it's known rather jokingly as God's Own Game. Except it's not really a joke when you consider how the sport was created in one of the alternative versions of Genesis.

(NB In my eyes the ECB will be first and foremost the England Cricket Board – not the European Central Bank).

The Creation of Cricket

1. In the beginning God created the heaven and the earth.
2. And the earth was void and without sport so he created a pitch with boundaries and it was long.*
3. And darkness was upon the pitch so God said, Let there be light.
4. And God called the light Day, and the darkness he called Night. And to play the sport he created Day in the Night, and God called this floodlights.
5. And God made marks upon on the pitch that divided the batsman from the bowler and God called them creases, and it was so.
6. And God said let the players defend wooden stumps surmounted by wooden cross pieces and this was the wicket, and it was good.
7. And God brought forth a willow staff and a red orb in order that the staff would strike the orb and send it into the firmament.
8. And during the flight of the red orb, it was deemed that batsmen would hurry the length of the pitch exchanging positions to score points.
9. And God said that the orb touching the ground before reaching the boundary shall bring forth four points, and the orb crossing the boundary without touching the

ground shall bring forth six points. And God called these points runs.

10. And God said if the orb is held captive while in flight or projected at the wooden stumps before the batsman takes shelter then he is declared out and God said, Howzat!

11. And God created more regulations and these were abundant and became the sanctified laws of the game which God called Cricket, and it was good.

12. And after he created Cricket God said let us make man in our image, after our likeness, and let him compete.

13. And God created two and twenty men and blessed them and God said unto them I have given you the pitch and the means and the laws. Go unto your crease and seek gratification in this sport.

14. And God saw everything that he had made, and he watched the play and behold, it was joyous.

15. And on the Seventh Day it rained and God called this a draw.

*44 cubits to be precise.

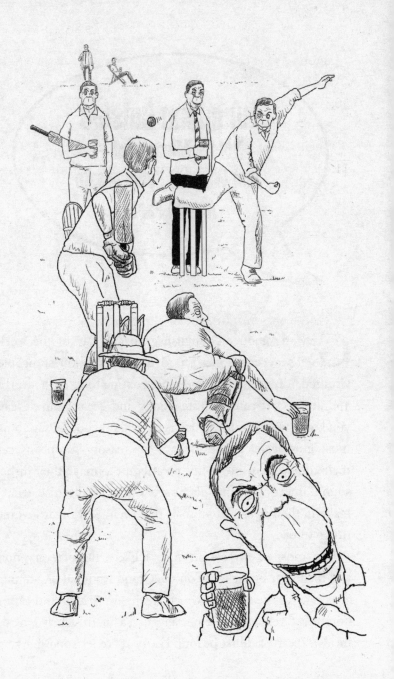

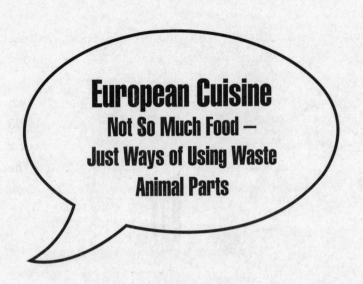

European Cuisine
Not So Much Food –
Just Ways of Using Waste
Animal Parts

Give me good old English grub any day of the week. It's decent honest food for decent honest people. Granted, it might not be the most exciting food in the world, and at times it can be quite stodgy and dreary, but at least you know what's in it – which is more than you can say about most European cuisine. In fact the reason Europeans call their cooking 'cuisine' is just an attempt to make their dishes sound interesting and glamorous, and to disguise what's really in them: parts of animals that even the Koreans would frown upon.

Like most of my countrymen I like a flutter every now and then. A fiver each way on the Grand National or a tenner on a nose at the Derby – which is why we British find eating horsemeat repugnant (especially if it's in mislabeled ready meals). It can of course be found in most French supermarkets, sold alongside pink veal, but then that probably doesn't surprise you. However eating horsemeat seems positively normal compared to other food that's popular across the continent.

Take, for example, something called Head Cheese, a dish popular in many European countries. This has nothing to do with cheese but everything to do with boiling the flesh of a sheep, pig or cow's head until it falls off, and then letting the whole mixture congeal into a gelatinous solid which is then served with a salad or in a sandwich. Think of it as a sort of primordial spam, but even less appealing.

And if you think that's bad, the worst chain pub steak and kidney pie tastes a million times better than some of these other foreign abominations…

Real European Dishes That Certainly Justify the Term 'Foreign Muck'

NAME	Beuschel
WHERE TO FIND IT	Austria
DESCRIPTION	This traditional dish from Vienna is better known as Lung Stew and is usually made with veal lungs and heart.
COMMENTS	With a recipe that usually begins 'separate the veal lung from the windpipe and gullet', is there any need to say more?

NAME	Casu marzu
WHERE TO FIND IT	Sardinia
DESCRIPTION	Sheep's milk cheese containing live maggots to help break down the cheese fats, soften it and imbue it with an unique flavour. The insect larvae are eaten with the cheese.
COMMENTS	Not so much a food as a biological weapon.

NAME	Beef tartare
WHERE TO FIND IT	Austria, Belgium, France, Denmark and Germany
DESCRIPTION	A patty of raw beef or horsemeat garnished with a raw egg.
COMMENTS	If you have a high resistance towards E. coli, Salmonella or vomiting, then this is the dish for you.

NAME	Véres hurka
WHERE TO FIND IT	Hungary
DESCRIPTION	Sausage usually made by boiling pig or cattle blood until it's congealed and then adding boiled and minced pig's organs and rice.
COMMENTS	Formerly looked upon as a meal of the poor, the dish should nowadays be looked upon as a meal for the desperate.

NAME	Blood eggs
WHERE TO FIND IT	Hungary
DESCRIPTION	Just what it is with the Hungarians and appalling food? Another of their traditional dishes, this one involves cooking scrambled eggs in pig's blood – traditionally, blood from the first pig killed that season.
COMMENTS	The slaughtered pig is considered more fortunate than those having to eat the actual meal.

NAME	Lutefisk
WHERE TO FIND IT	Denmark, Finland and Sweden
DESCRIPTION	An aged whitefish described as being 'glutinous in texture' and having a 'pungent, offensive odour'. If that wasn't bad enough, Lutefisk is often described as being 'infamously unpleasant'.
COMMENTS	Those experiencing the Lutefisk aroma for the first time have compared the sensation as like 'being hit with CS gas'.

NAME	Criadillas
WHERE TO FIND IT	Spain
DESCRIPTION	Fried testicles of prize bulls sometimes presented on a Spanish menu under the dish's more innocuous name, 'bull fries'.
COMMENTS	Not many chefs get past the first line of the recipe: 'Remove the membrane from the testicles by gently cutting it.' NB Some Spaniards think that eating the testicles of prized bulls makes you brave and more masculine. In reality it just makes you unsettled and more nauseous.

NAME	Polšja obara
WHERE TO FIND IT	Slovenia
DESCRIPTION	A thick dormice soup or stew made with potatoes, spices, apple vinegar and, of course, dormice.
COMMENTS	There are few dormice in Slovenia. Not because of efficient pest control or deforestation, but because the locals find them so damned tasty.

NAME	Lappkok
WHERE TO FIND IT	Sweden and Finland
DESCRIPTION	Dumplings made from reindeer blood, and mixed with wheat or rye flour.
COMMENTS	The genius who came up with this dish probably wondered if it were still possible to make it any more abhorrent. The answer was a resounding 'yes', which is why it's traditionally served with reindeer bone marrow.

NAME	Cockscomb
WHERE TO FIND IT	Italy
DESCRIPTION	Cockscombs are the floppy red fleshy things on top of roosters' heads that look like weird upside down gloves. Why anyone would have a) ever wondered what they tasted like and b) decided they should be an important component of Italian stews and a sauce for tagliatelle defies belief.
COMMENTS	The tips of the cockscomb are described as 'slightly gelatinous, with hints of delicate frog-leg flavour'.

UKIP and Dating

Research has shown that UKIP members and supporters tend to enjoy long marriages. They might be loveless and unfulfilling after the children leave home – when you and your wife realise the only thing you have in common is having nothing in common – but nonetheless, they are long. Very long.

Sometimes, however, your partner gets the bit between their teeth and, influenced by what she reads in weekly celebrity magazines or by completing Facebook quizzes like 'So You Think You're Happy?' or 'Could You Do Better?', she decides to leave. In most cases, when a UKIPer gets divorced it's usually because of what's called 'irreconcilable differences'. In non-legal terms this is when your wife accuses you of being a 'unrelenting bore', spending too much of your time bell-ringing, glass blowing, brass rubbing, collecting

Star Wars figures or Nazi memorabilia, re-enacting English Civil War battles, or constructing 1:72 scale models of Second World War armoured fighting vehicles. Occasionally, though, you'll just find yourself replaced by someone taller, fitter and usually slightly swarthier and younger, who bears more than a passing resemblance to Enrique Inglesias and who, you're told, 'knows how to fulfil my womanly needs'.

Whatever the reason for separating, you'll find it traumatic and a time of mixed emotions. On the one hand, it's good to have newfound freedom – no one to tell you what to do, what to wear, or to constantly point out every single one of your many flaws – but on the other hand, even UKIPers need company; someone to look after them, cook for them and accompany them to Beer Festivals or Genesis reunion concerts.

The Best Places For UKIPers To Meet Women

Beer festivals
For: You'll automatically have something in common.
Against: She'll probably be dumpy, unkempt and look like she was an extra in *The Hobbit*.

Science-fiction conventions
For: She might resemble Number Six from *Battlestar Galactica*.
Against: She'll inevitably resemble Emperor Palpatine from *Return of the Jedi*.

A pub or bar

For: There's a chance an attractive, normal woman will find you fascinating, charming, interesting and enigmatically handsome.

Against: This will never happen.

A fashionable club or disco

For: Any woman you meet is likely to be young, sexy and really fit.

Against: You think you'll be allowed past the velvet rope?

A DIY superstore

For: Women wandering the aisles alone are likely to be single and your friendly, helpful advice on caulking or grouting can be a good conversation opener.

Against: Loitering for half a day in the drill bits aisle is likely to get you arrested or at least thrown out.

Art gallery

For: Many single women visit galleries to admire or study the beauty of the paintings. You can impress them with your knowledge of Old Dutch masters.

Against: The chances are you'll get Van Gogh mixed up with Van Halen.

At work

For: You've probably already met all the contenders for a possible relationship.

Against: They've already met you.

Introduction by a friend

For: Your potential partner will have already been pre-vetted and qualified.

Against: You'll need to have a friend.

Party

For: Alcohol, music, mystery and wildness… all the ingredients for a successful evening.

Against: When was the last time someone invited you to a party?

Party conference

For: Prejudice, right-wing leanings and being socially awkward… you'll have so much in common!

Against: Seriously. Have you seen the women at UKIP party conferences?

Understanding Online Dating

Where UKIPers have found some success in meeting new partners is in online dating. The biggest advantage over old-style Lonely Hearts newspaper ads is that you can see your prospective partner before you start entering into a conversation. The biggest disadvantage however is that she can do the same (which is an issue if you bear more than a passing resemblance to David Mellor). And similar to Lonely Hearts ads, you'll be entering a world of strange shorthand and acronyms, so it's vital you understand the right 'trigger' phrases to attract a like-minded soul mate.

Useful acronyms for UKIPers to use in their ads

SUKIPBDJM	Single UKIPer but don't judge me
IDTM	Is desperate to meet
IRRDTM	Is really, really desperate to meet
DB	Decent bloke
DysB	Dysfunctional bloke
FL	Fun loving (if your idea of fun involves camping, canvassing or Sudoku)
GSOH	Good sense of humour (as long as you like Monty Python)
OC	Own caravan
LWM	Lives with mother

GL	Good looking (if your ideal man is out of shape with thinning hair and bad teeth)
RAD	Real ale drinker
SS	Social smoker (not to be confused with the SchutzStaffel, the Nazi paramilitary organisation; see OMF)
FOTG	Fan of *Top Gear*
WB	Well built (beer belly)
OMF	Open-minded female (someone who doesn't think it's odd that I like to dress up as member of the Waffen-SS in private and have people address me as 'Obergruppenführer')
IIL	Inexperienced in love (makes *The 40-Year-Old Virgin* look like Hugh Hefner)
LTT	Loves to travel (as long as we stay in the UK)
RPP	Racially pure preferred
45	57
55	64

GOOD CHAT-UP LINES

- I want to do to you what David Cameron wants to do to the poor working class.
- I've got a five-year plan and it includes you. But it doesn't have to be five years. One night works for me.
- Immigration numbers aren't the only thing that's rising.
- You're hotter than global warming (which, incidentally, is a fallacy).
- You had me at 'rigorous cuts in foreign aid'.
- I'm so depressed about the Public Sector Net Borrowing I really don't think I should spend tonight alone.
- Let's play NHS reform. Or as I call it, 'doctors and nurses'.
- I want to drill you as if I'm looking for shale gas.
- Hello. I'm conducting a poll. What's your name? What's your phone number? Are you free next Saturday?
- Let me show you the size of my majority.
- You make me harder than the EU rules about harmonization of the gross national product.
- Wanna go back to my place and form a coalition?
- You've got your man-date.
- How would you like to feel my powerful pressure group?
- If taking you home tonight was like a referendum, I'd definitely vote 'YES!'
- No, it's not a rolled-up copy of our energy policy booklet in my pocket. I'm just pleased to see you.

- Going home without you tonight would be a contravention against my human rights (although I need to make it clear that we want to repeal the Human Rights Act).
- I'm a campaigner in the streets but a tiger between the sheets.
- You must be an Islamic suicide bomber because you look like you've come here straight from heaven.
- Hey darlin', let's play border control. You can be the door to foreign workers and I'll slam you all night long.

MAIL-ORDER BRIDES

If you're a UKIP member or supporter you'll be very familiar with this topic. Half the people with a view on the subject of mail-order brides say finding a partner this way indicates you're a desperate, unattractive failure with low self-esteem and virtually no social skills who just wants a subservient wife to make him feel better about his pathetic sad existence. The other half tends to agree. But whatever your situation, you should be fully aware of the pros and cons.

Advantage of a mail-order bride
This might be the only way you'll find someone who actually wants to marry you.

<u>Disadvantage of a mail-order bride</u>
They're foreign.

Once you can come to terms with this, there is an upside; the women tend to come from impoverished backgrounds like the Ukraine, Belarus or Thailand so 'splashing the cash' around them usually only means waving about a fiver, an HMV gift card or some luncheon vouchers.

<u>WARNING</u>
Most mail-order brides are just after two things: a visa and your money. Watch out for these signs:

5 clues that your mail-order bride is a gold digger
1. You sometimes wonder what she sees in a short, overweight, balding man with his own house and caravan.
2. She crumples your love poem into a ball and yells, 'I wanted a pair of Jimmy Choos, not this shit!'
3. Her pet name for you is 'Sugar Daddy' not 'Hunny Bunny'.
4. She violently disagrees with the adage that 'money can't buy you love'.
5. She's sucking you dry... and not in the good way.

Freedom of Choice #2
Fox Hunting

L ook. I love animals as much as the next man but I also love freedom. That's freedom from government intervention and freedom for toffs to chase foxes to within an inch of their lives. And then kill them.

But I'm not saying I actively support fox hunting. In fact I'm very, very careful not to say that as I'm well aware that 80 per cent of the electorate still supports Blair's 2004 ban. What I'm in favour of is local councils and communities using the democratic process, the backbone of this great country of ours, to ask their constituents what they want. It's that simple. If those in favour of hunting win the vote, they can hunt; if they lose, they can't – and no matter what the result is, I don't show my hand.

It's a win-win-win situation!

And although I'm not nailing my colours to the mast I would just point out that there are quite a few arguments in support of lifting the fox-hunting ban. Not that I'm agreeing with that of course.

Tally Ho!

Arguments in Support of Fox Hunting

Hunting is an essential part of traditional rural life.
Like an engrained mistrust of outsiders and political views that date back to the 1820s, who wants to see these go?

Protesters don't understand hunting
Hunt protestors are usually ill-informed since they only turn up before a hunt or long after it's over. This means they have no actual idea about what's involved. How can they make a rational case against hunting if they haven't actually seen blood-thirsty hounds ripping a fox to shreds before a huntsman holds its dripping carcass aloft so that the dogs can continue snapping at it?

Hunting provides jobs
Discounting those who have other full-time or part-time employment in the countryside, it's estimated that overturning the hunting ban would provide an additional 180 jobs throughout the whole of the UK.

Hunting is natural
Man has always hunted: if not for animals, then for his keys. In addition, death is an unavoidable part of nature, and if they weren't hunted and killed mercilessly, foxes would die of natural causes anyway.

The fox doesn't suffer
After it's flushed out and cornered, hounds can rip a fox to bloody shreds in about a minute. And if it's still breathing after that, a few swift blows to the head with a shovel will soon put it out of its misery.

It's good for the hounds
Every chase is fraught with danger for the dogs. From avoiding being hit by cars or trains, to injuring themselves in quarries, gravel pits or on barbed wire... the thrill of the hunt adds some excitement into what would otherwise be sedate, safe, comfortable lives in the country as beloved family pets.

Foxes terrorise the countryside
Foxes can roam the countryside in packs, with their 'kill zones' extending as far as 250 miles, attacking and maiming sheep and chickens – and sometimes humans too.
Or is that wolves?

**Great Britons No. 2
Robert Falcon Scott**

What a bloke! Not just a Royal Navy officer and polar explorer, but from what I know about him, a gentleman too. Scott encapsulates all that's great about Britain; a spirit for adventure, stoicism, bravery, determination and, ultimately, failure. But let's not dwell on the failure for too long. He should be commended for leading the second team to the South Pole and was only beaten by Norwegian Roald Amundsen because Norway wasn't (and isn't) in the EU. If it had have been, then by the time Amundsen had filled out the required 256-page 'Polar Exploration Licence' and the accompanying 72-page 'Husky Permit', and then conducted a comprehensive risk assessment of his mission, then Scott would have been there and back before you could say, 'frostbite'.

It's not a well-known fact but Scott was not just a brave explorer, he was also one of the earliest climate change sceptics. Like us, he doubted the rate at which the polar ice caps were melting and that mankind influenced climate change. If Scott were alive today then he'd probably be in UKIP, possibly even leading our campaign to repeal the 2008 Climate Change Act and to abandon its legally-binding targets for reducing emissions of greenhouse gases that costs the UK economy £18 billion a year.

Anyway, he persuaded the Royal Geographic Society to back his first expedition on board the Discovery in 1901 and he came back in 1904 a national hero. The expedition was quite uneventful although halfway through, fellow explorer Ernest Shackleton left on a relief ship. The official line was that he'd had a breakdown but I think it was because they came to blows over damning evidence that carbon dioxide levels were not responsible for significant warming or weather effects.

Despite Scott's invaluable findings he was still a lone voice among the climate change dissenters and displaying true British resolve to find the truth he set off again in 1910, this time aboard the Terra Nova. It was an expedition that would ultimately cost the lives of Scott and his men in March 1912 when fierce blizzards trapped them until their supplies ran out. In another example of honour and selfless sacrifice that only the British can demonstrate, Scott's colleague Captain Oates voluntarily left the tent in order to save rations for his colleagues. His last brave words as he stepped outside into a violent snowstorm were, 'I may be some time.'

Those words are as relevant today as they were a hundred years ago. It's what Nick Clegg's going to say after the election when asked, 'So when will you get back into Government?'

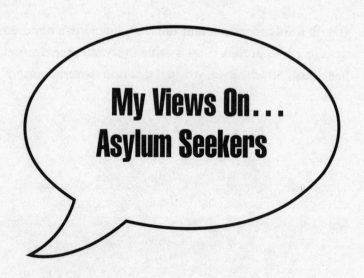

My Views On...
Asylum Seekers

Asylum seekers go by many names: boat people, illegal immigrants, sponging stowaways, lorry chassis-hanging freeloaders. But whatever you call them, under international law anyone has the right to apply for asylum in any country that signed the 1951 UN Refugee Convention – and stay there until the authorities have assessed their claim. And guess what. The UK signed it. In ink.

Now I'm not against asylum seekers per se; in fact I can sympathise with everything they've gone through. I've been persecuted and ill-treated too – although in my case it's by the media, not by secret state police or lawless militia – but the principle is exactly the same.

What I get enraged about is asylum seekers coming over, waltzing right into this marvellous country of ours and getting benefits from day one without making any contribution of their own. Many of them claim they can't work because they still suffer from post-traumatic shock after seeing their families slaughtered in some racial genocide or they've had limbs removed by machetes in tribal attacks. Well I say, 'boo hoo'. Man up and deal with it.

They should take a leaf out of the book of some of the most famous British refugees, the Pilgrim Fathers. Sure they were religiously persecuted but they didn't get all uppity about it. They just sailed all the way across the Atlantic to North America to make a new home but more importantly, they did it legally; there was no trying to sneak in when no one was looking. And don't talk to me about hardship. They were at sea for sixty-five days, not hiding in the back of some container from Calais to Dover for just a few hours.

And when they eventually did arrive they had no one giving them handouts or a council house. They worked hard to build a new community and guess what, they didn't form some sort of ghetto and keep themselves to themselves. They were happy to mix with the Red Indians and share things with them. The Indians gave them maize and the settlers gave them plague infected blankets. It all worked well.

If you're an asylum seeker and you're reading this (which might be difficult as you probably don't understand English or you may have lost your sight in a gas attack by the tyrannical regime you escaped from) there's a lesson here. Be positive, give something back to the community but above all, stop griping. Yes I'm sure your three-day walk to freedom through a minefield was exhausting or the fact you were adrift in a boat for a week without food or water was gruelling but you're not unique. Thousands have said the same thing. And yes, I'm sure you did get tortured but just remember, you got it for free. Lots of people here pay good money to get slapped or have electrodes attached to their genitals.

Just ask anyone on the Tory back bench.

40 Reasons Why People Are Voting for UKIP

Look, at the end of the day I don't really care if you support UKIP because you agree with our policies on exiting the EU, points-based immigration, decreasing foreign aid, increasing inward investment, scrapping HS2, improving the NHS, helping the elderly, or because you once ate some soft French cheese and it gave you the runs.

When it comes down to it a vote's a vote, so I'll be happy if any of these reasons strike a chord with other members of the electorate…

1. 'The metric system makes my shoe size a 44 and that sounds like I have the same size feet as Ronald McDonald.'

2. 'Last Saturday night my local A&E was absolutely full of immigrants! After getting drunk and falling over, one gave me an X-ray and one bandaged my arm.'

3. 'I don't know what Polski Sklep means and I'm scared.'

4. 'Jif was pressured by European countries to change its name. Now every time I ask the man in the corner shop if he has Cif, he punches me.'

5. 'I heard all Romanians are vampires.'

6. 'Because what this country needs are scapegoats.'

7. 'Nearly all of the major wars have involved foreigners. You can't trust them.'

8. 'I want to experience what it was like to live in pre-war Germany.'

9. 'Because I went to the countryside last autumn and most of the leaves were brown.'

10. 'I heard that Slovenians are responsible for coastal erosion.'

11. 'Because I want to support the Ku Klux Klan but I live in Thanet, not Alabama.'

12. 'I went to Nando's the other day and one in four chairs was facing Mecca.'

13. 'I nearly choked on a French Golden Delicious apple.'

14. 'I stepped on a Lego brick with my bare foot.'

15. 'The Romanian community has a high level of organised crime. I know; I've watched *The Godfather* three times.'

16. 'I never forgave the Tories for allowing Dime bars to become Daim. One day it's confectionery. The next it's German stormtroopers hammering on our doors to drag us off to death camps.'

17. 'I think my chippy is using Halal potatoes.'

18. 'I've got too much self-respect to vote for the BNP.'

19. 'I get all my eco-political insights from my mates down the pub.'

20. 'I had German measles when I was six.'

21. 'It's far easier to blame someone else for my own inadequacies and failures.'

22. 'I tried to find a bag of Skittles at my newsagent last week but all I could see were loads of bars of dark chocolate.'

23. 'You can really trust a man who admires Russian presidents who are half-naked homophobic Cold War fetishists.'

24. 'I tried to yodel and strained my voice.'

25. 'Because human rights are so overrated.'

26. 'I wasted £9 going to see the remake of *The Italian Job*. It was terrible and, probably, so is their country.'

27. 'I want my MP to be someone edgy, who looks like he might suddenly say something really, really offensive about minority groups.'

28. 'Those Russian meerkats are taking all our jobs.'

29. 'I saw two men talking in Starbucks last Wednesday. I couldn't hear them but I think they were planning their wedding.'

30. 'The spread of multiculturalism will mean my favourite heavy metal bands will be forced to play steel drums and didgeridoos.'

31. 'Because we allow foreigners to waltz in here and take all the low-paid menial jobs. If I actually wanted a low-paid menial job, I'd be bloody furious.'

32. 'Nigel smokes and I smoke, so he must be a really good bloke.'

33. 'My Alfa Romeo got a puncture and I was late for work.'

34. 'Because the money that's going on housing benefits for refugees could be funding the child allowance for my twelve children from five different husbands.'

35. 'I run an illegal dog-fighting ring, have a Union Jack flag covering the side of my bungalow and the word England tattooed down one calf.'

36. 'I really hate Björk, A-ha and Aqua – and they're all foreign.'

37. 'Because I love having a smug sense of superiority over anyone who speaks with an accent.'

38. 'Because the EU will make us eat all the Grand National runners.'

39. 'I got really sunburned when I went to Benidorm.'

40. 'I don't really believe in rational, balanced arguments.'

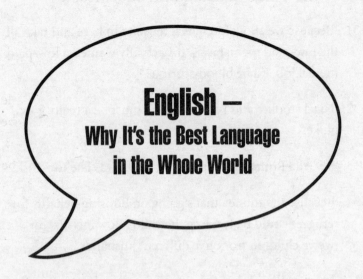

English –
Why It's the Best Language in the Whole World

Each year the EU spends €330m a year (that's £256m in real money) on translation services. There are 24 official EU languages but not surprisingly, by a long, long way, most documents end up being translated into English. That means the UK tax payer is subsidising foreign civil servants, politicians and policy makers who frankly can't be bothered to learn English. It's deplorable, especially when you consider that the English language is superior for a whole host of recognisable reasons:

10 Reasons Why English is Bloody Marvellous

1. English has the largest vocabulary of any language in the world. The Eskimos may have 23 words for snow but we have 87 racial slurs for foreigners.

2. It's so versatile that you can alter the meaning of some phrases just by changing one single letter, e.g. 'Jean-Claude Juncker is a runt.'

3. Hollywood catchphrases just wouldn't be that memorable if they weren't in English. Take Arnie's classic, 'I'll be back!'. Would it have the same impact in Lithuanian?: 'Grišiu!' Or would you still laugh at 'Surely you can't be serious. I am serious, and don't call me Shirley' if it was in Danish?: 'Sikkert kan du ikke være alvorlige. Jeg er seriøs og ikke kalder mig Shirley'.

4 You don't need to worry about remembering things like a hat being masculine but a roller skate being feminine.

5. There are so many irregular verbs that you can have a real laugh when foreigners say things like, 'He selled me his car,' or 'Yesterday I goed to the cinema.'

6. Ask yourself how many *X Factor* winners sang in their native Estonian or Hungarian (actually, I'll save you the bother. The answer is none). If you want to be a reality TV singing sensation like Steve Brookstein you need to sing in English.

7. Spoken English sounds a million times more pleasant than spoken German, Flemish or Dutch, where even a simple sentence sounds like someone getting angry while vomiting.

8. Imagine if Bulgarian was the language of the Internet. You'd have to type 'Ким Кардашян гола плячка снимки' just to see 'Kim Kardashian nude booty photos'.

9. English is very succinct. Sentences translated from

English into other languages take up at least 30 per cent more space, saving ream upon ream of paper.

10. Spoken English has many subtle nuances to express a wide range of emotions, unlike German for example, which is far better suited to shouting orders rather than expressing affection or being funny.

The 7 Most Overrated Foreign Tourist Attractions

Whether you live in the capital or not, you have to agree that London has some of the best tourist attractions in the world, and especially some of the best in Europe. Sure, Paris has the Eiffel Tower, Berlin has the Reichstag, Rome has the Coliseum and Madrid has… well, Madrid has absolutely no great landmarks. At all. OK, it has museums and plazas and a park – but that's it. Anyway, even without Madrid, mainland Europe's tourist attractions can't hold a candle to their equivalents in London. It's no wonder then that we're overrun by tourists. And by tourists I mean temporary immigrants.

St Paul's Cathedral

Now this is what you call a cathedral! It's one of the most iconic buildings in London and has survived not just hundreds of thousands of annoying tourists but the might of the German Luftwaffe. Inside there's a great crypt that's home to tombs and memorials of some of the nation's greatest conquering heroes, including Admiral Lord Nelson and the Duke of Wellington. Visitors

can also climb up to the Golden Gallery to enjoy breathtaking views across the best city in the world. St Paul's took just 35 years to build – a textbook example of British efficiency (see below).

La Sagrada Família, Barcelona

Antoni Gaudí's Church of the Sacred Family is often described as 'an astonishing structure' and 'a magical masterpiece', but

far more accurate descriptions would be 'tourist infested building site' and 'ill-conceived pastiche'. This cathedral is universally heralded as a masterpiece of engineering, but the fact that it was started in 1882 and is *still* under construction is more of a testament to the general laziness of Spanish builders.

The London Eye

The most popular paid tourist attraction in the UK, the London Eye stands over 440 feet tall and is Europe's largest Ferris wheel – so put that in your pipe Jean-Claude Juncker! It's also one of the world's tallest observation wheels, offering awe-inspiring views over London's world-famous landmarks such as Big Ben, Buckingham Palace, The Shard, Trafalgar Square, St Paul's Cathedral, the Gherkin and Canary Wharf. God, it makes me proud just listing these places.

Eiffel Tower, Paris

This monument should only be looked at, not visited. If you foolishly decide to ascend to the top, be prepared to experience security checks that make Inspector Clouseau look like the pinnacle of efficiency, lifts that travel (appropriately enough) at a snail's pace and an observation deck that's so cramped it gives you a great opportunity to experience French irony: an abundance of signs that warn against pickpockets amid acute overcrowding that makes their job simple. And when you do eventually reach the top and look out over a sprawling grey Paris, the uninspiring view just adds to your disappointment.

The National Gallery

Housing one of the best collections of paintings in the world the National Gallery believes in quality over quantity. The Louvre, take note. Its carefully curated collection of 2,300 paintings includes masterpieces on display by Van Gogh, Turner, Da Vinci, Reubens, Monet and Rembrandt to name but a few. What's more, these works of art belong to the British public so entrance here is free. Again, the Louvre, take note.

Musée du Louvre, Paris

Recognised the world over for the completely out-of-character large glass pyramid in its main courtyard, and for its appallingly sluggish ticket office, the Louvre displays 35,000 works of art. However 92 per cent of its visitors just go to see one: the Mona Lisa. If you follow in their footsteps (and you'll have to, as the dawdling crowds prevent you from overtaking them) prepare to be disappointed. The portrait is tiny, not just because it's far smaller than you think, but because there's always at

least twenty other people in front of you stopping you from getting close. It's said that Mona Lisa's smile was enigmatic. Your look of utter disappointment, though, will be obvious.

Nelson's Column

Overlooking Trafalgar Square and proudly standing nearly 170 feet tall, this great monument commemorates Admiral Horatio Nelson, one of the world's greatest ever naval commanders who defeated – in fact, smashed – the fleets not just of the French and Spanish but also the Danes and the Norwegians. As if the statue itself isn't enough of a reminder of British naval superiority, the square pedestal at the foot of the column features four bronze panels cast from captured French cannons.

The Little Mermaid, Copenhagen

You can't blame yourself if you're not utterly disillusioned with this tourist attraction. The big hint is the world 'Little'. Erected in 1913 to honour Hans Christian Andersen's fairy tale, this 4'1" sculpture should be more accurately named 'The Remarkably Underwhelming Mermaid', or 'The

Exceptionally Unimposing Mermaid'. You'll find it at the harbour, set against an ugly industrial backdrop and naval yard. All you have to do is follow the disappointed cries of 'Is that it?'

Marble Arch

When John Nash designed Marble Arch in 1827 he wanted to create something similar to, but not as rubbish as, the triumphal Arch of Constantine in Rome. This colossal monument was originally constructed on the Mall as an entrance to Buckingham Palace, but it was painstakingly moved, brick by brick, to Hyde Park in 1851. A perfect example of British ingenuity and workmanship, and remember: this was a time before East European builders.

Brandenburg Gate, Berlin

Many people consider this former 18th century City Gate, commissioned by King Frederick William II of Prussia, to be the primary symbol of Berlin's colourful and turbulent history. They are wrong. Very wrong. It's more the primary symbol of Berlin's ability to completely over-restore one of its most historic attractions so that it looks like it was built in 1991

not 1791. Worth a visit only if you want to have your photo taken with out-of-work actors posing as Russian soldiers, or to buy smelly currywurst sausages from unhygienic-looking food carts.

Tower of London

One of the world's most famous fortresses with a rich history that dates back to its construction in 1078. Since then it's seen service as a royal palace, a prison, an armoury, a treasury, and even a zoo. How many foreign attractions can match that? Not many, I can tell you! Today uniformed beefeaters protect the magnificent and priceless Crown Jewels which are on display for visitors to see. The Tower is said to be haunted by the ghost of Anne Boleyn carrying her head under her arm – and that's not something you see every day.

Leaning Tower of Pisa

An example of typical Italian workmanship in the only city in the world where a tourist attraction has been created out of subsidence.

Vinopolis

If, like me, you love wine, you'll love Vinopolis! Covering a massive 2.5 acres and located just five minutes from London Bridge, it's the perfect place to learn about the history of wine but more importantly, indulge in some

wine tasting. Whether you're a social drinker, a wine connoisseur or a raging alcoholic, you'll have a great time here (though you may not remember it).

The Acropolis, Athens

Rising above Athens and containing the remains of several ancient temples including the Parthenon, as soon as you hear the words 'sacred rock' or 'ruins' attached to an attraction, you know it's going to be a disappointment. The Greeks have the same concept of ticketing and organisation as they do of responsible government expenditure, so to get to the

top you need to survive an ill-tempered queue with no shade, and at least a 30-minute dangerously overcrowded trek and almost guaranteed heat stroke. Is that really how you want to spend a holiday?

Garlic: Nature's Atrocity

'*Do not eat garlic or onions; for their smell will reveal
that you are a peasant.*'

– MIGUEL DE CERVANTES, SPANISH NOVELIST
(AND A FAR BETTER JUDGE OF FOODS THAN AN AUTHOR).

Garlic, or to give it its Latin name *allium sativum* (literally,
'onion's stinky cousin') became popular in European
cuisine after chefs in France, Italy, Greece and Spain first
discovered its most valuable property: its ability to disguise
the taste of revolting Mediterranean dishes.

In addition to this essential role, garlic lovers maintain that
this vegetable has many beneficial effects and call it 'nature's
pharmacy'. They claim it lowers cholesterol and blood pressure
and is a good remedy for colds and flu, but since garlic is also

associated with the power to ward off vampires, it's probably best to take any health claims with a pinch of salt.*

Fans, however, acknowledge that garlic does polarise people and compare it to Marmite. Yet this analogy presents garlic in an inaccurate, favourable light.

It's actually more like raw liver. Everyone hates it.

*which would actually be far tastier.

Garlic FAQs

What is the main property of garlic?
Its use as an effective contraceptive.

Does garlic have a place in every kitchen?
Yes. Under or behind somewhere heavy or inaccessible, or in the swing bin.

Can I eat raw garlic?
Of course, if you want to experience what it's like to lick a live battery.

Is there anything worse than the smell of garlic?
Yes. Its taste.

What can I serve to complement a dish containing garlic?
A mug of Listerine.

Is it true that the slaves who built the pyramids in Ancient Egypt chewed on garlic to give them raw energy?
You're an idiot.

OK, but according to many religions, when the Devil was cast out of the Garden of Eden, garlic sprang up where his left foot had touched the ground. Is that true?
That's probably more like it.

The Eurovision Song Contest – Why It Should Have Nil Points

It's difficult to know what inspires more hatred in me: that this horrifying event should ever exist in the first place, or that it provides yet another excuse for Graham Norton to appear on our screens. A talent show for the untalented, this is state-funded propaganda at its very worst. When Terry Wogan hosted it, no one took it seriously. It was a bit of silly fun and he took the piss out of the whole thing. In recent years, though, it's turned into a vicious, prejudiced political forum, a sort of EU Parliament but with bad songs, where everyone gangs up against Great Britain for a) existing and b) having a world-beating musical legacy that includes the Beatles, Showaddywaddy and Phil Collins.

And in no event at all (unless it involves bauxite mining or ploughing) should you ever have to hear the words, 'It looks like Azerbaijan are the clear favourites'…

5 Things Wrong With the Eurovision Song Contest

It's irresponsible for East European countries to enter

Estonia, Macedonia, Belarus, Croatia, the Ukraine, Moldova, Latvia… Shouldn't these countries be concentrating on keeping an eye on their grain harvest or regulating working conditions for their prostitutes, rather than investing resources that they can ill-afford into entering the contest?

Everyone just votes for their neighbours

It's no coincidence that Latvia routinely awards top marks to Lithuania, Cyprus regularly throws a few points Greece's way and Bulgaria is the biggest supporter of Romania. It seems the Eurovision Song Contest is less about choosing the best overall song and more about casting votes on the basis of geography, ideology or having similar dopey-looking national costumes.

The songs are appalling

If music is a universal language then the Eurovision Song Contest demonstrates the universal language of shockingly bad music. Supporters point out that it provides an opportunity to hear musical styles you might otherwise not be exposed to. That's correct. Where else could you sit down in front of your TV on a Saturday night and hear Moldavan reggae, Hungarian rap, Slovenian techno or Albanian blues. What's more, the contest features Song titles! With lots! Of exclamation marks!

(NB The balalaika will never, ever be an effective substitute for an electric guitar.)

The singers are appalling

Outside of a Little Mix concert, the Eurovision Song Contest holds the monopoly on singers with a complete lack of charm, charisma and any ability to hold a tune. Here you can watch Armenia's uglier version of Duran Duran, the Maltese Leo Sayer, the Icelandic Bee Gees or a singer from Georgia who looks and sounds like a poor man's Chesney Hawkes who's sold 60 million albums in Turkey.

It's an insidious way of promoting a united Europe

On the face of it, it's a harmless piece of light entertainment but scratch the veneer of talentless acts and you'll see a selection of angst-ridden and worthy songs about unity, peace, harmony, or lighting a candle: performances accompanied by scenes of hideous rampant nationalism that make the Nuremberg rallies look like a WI coffee morning.

UKIP Fairy Tales No.1
Cleggio

Gepetto Cameron put down his paintbrush and looked at the small wooden figure sitting before him in his cluttered workshop. 'I was going to call you Pinocchio but you are so absolutely lifeless and wooden that I will call you Cleggio,' he said aloud.

'If only you had a personality,' he said to himself. 'If only you were real rather than just my puppet.'

Gepetto put Cleggio on a shelf, turned off the lights and went to bed.

That night, however, when Gepetto was fast asleep, the Blue Fairy swept in through an open window and brought Cleggio to life, telling him that if he proved himself truthful and unselfish he would become a real politician.

The next morning Gepetto cried with joy. Somehow his

wish for Cleggio had come true. He sent him off to private school so he could be better educated, but on his way Cleggio was led astray and joined a circus called the European Union.

After performing for the boss of the circus, Jean-Claude Juncker, Cleggio found himself locked in a birdcage, trapped and lost. His plaintive cries for help however were heard by the Blue Fairy, who appeared once more.

'Oh Cleggio,' she said despondently, looking at his predicament. 'Why, oh why, did you join the EU Circus?'

'Because it's good for our country and the British people,' Cleggio replied earnestly.

'You don't seriously believe that?' asked the Blue Fairy, rolling her eyes.

'Most definitely,' Cleggio said, adding, 'And if we left it would be unpatriotic!'

The Blue Fairy couldn't believe what she was hearing. 'If John Humphrys had heard that, he would have been astonished,' she commented, and went on, 'But what would actually happen if Britain left the EU?'

'Mass unemployment. Three million jobs depend on our continued membership,' Cleggio stated.

And just then, something very unusual happened.

His nose began to grow.

Cleggio continued. 'Without membership of the EU and their cooperation hundreds of murderers and paedophiles could enter Britain.'

His nose grew some more. It was now about four inches long.

'Leaving would make many working people poorer, and no one would take the UK seriously on the world stage.'

By now Cleggio's nose was six inches long. The Blue Fairy couldn't take her eyes off of it.

'You certainly know your facts,' she said. 'But there is one more thing I need to ask you.'

'Of course,' said Cleggio.

'Do you really believe you can win the argument to remain in the EU and that the Lib Dems will remain a credible force in British politics?'

'Most definitely,' said Cleggio smiling, as his nose passed cleanly through the bars of his cage and the tip almost touched the adjacent wall.

The End.

German Humour: It's No Laughing Matter

I don't know if you've ever been to Bavaria, a region in south-east Germany renowned for oompah bands, beer halls, lederhosen, sausages and right wing leanings masquerading as a traditional way of life. It's quite a jolly place really. Anyway, I was there recently on MEP business and ended up in a comedy club with some colleagues. Now 'German humour' is as much an oxymoron as Dutch cuisine, Estonian charm, Greek prudence or Polish glamour but I thought I'd sit it out with a few beers.

Now I don't believe in stereotyping a whole nation but it won't come as any surprise to you when I say that the Germans understand humour as much as the Hungarians understand fashion. These are the five funniest jokes I heard that evening:

Joke 1

Why can't you get aspirin in the jungle?
Because it would not be financially viable to attempt to sell pharmaceuticals in the largely unpopulated rainforest.

Joke 2

My dog has no nose.
How does it smell?
It's okay. He has got one, really.

Joke 3

Knock, knock.
Who's there?
It's me. Sorry, I forgot my keys again.

Joke 4

An Englishman, an Italian, and a German walk into a bar. The German says to the bartender: 'These are my friends, one is an Englishman and one is Italian. I am German.'

Joke 5

How many Germans does it take to change a light bulb?
One.

As I had to endure ninety minutes of this sub-Chuckle Brothers routine, I thought I'd get my own back with some genuinely funny British humour that I know the Germans would appreciate:

Q: Why are there so many tree-lined streets and leafy lanes in France?

A: Germans like to march in the shade.

Q: Why do they bury Germans 20 metres underground?

A: Because deep down they are really nice.

Q: What is the difference between Christianity and National Socialism?

A: In Christianity, one guy died for all the others.

Q: How do you get rid of aristocratic Germans?

A: Von by von.

Q: What's the difference between a German and a shopping trolley?

A: A shopping trolley has a mind of its own.

Q: Have you heard about the new German-Chinese restaurant?

A: The food is great, but an hour later, you're hungry for power.

Q: What does a German politician have in common with a German porn star's mouth?

A: They're both full of shit.

Q: What did the German kid say when he pushed his brother off the cliff?
A: 'Look mum! No Hans!'

Q: What do you call a pissed-off German?
A: A sauerkraut.

Q: How does the recipe for German chocolate cake begin?
A: First, invade ze kitchen.

Q: Did you hear about the winner of the German beauty contest?
A: Me neither.

Q: How did the current Pope get elected?
A: He was the first one to put his towel on the balcony.

Knock, Knock.
Who's there?
Gestapo.
Gestapo who?
Ve vill ask zee questions!

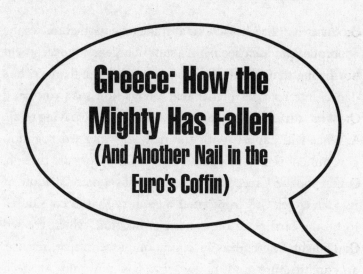

Greece: How the Mighty Has Fallen (And Another Nail in the Euro's Coffin)

Sure, it must have seemed like a really great idea in 2001 when Greece became the 12th country to adopt the euro. It was a time for celebration… one of the biggest steps in European integration that promised the Eurozone countries great prosperity. Except in this case they mistook the words 'economic growth' for 'catastrophic financial collapse'.

Ten years after it adopted the euro Greece received its first massive bailout… The writing was on the wall really; it's no coincidence that the word 'economic' and the word 'chaos' are both derived from their language.

So why did it all go wrong? Well this is book is called *The World According to Nigel Farage*, not 'The Geo-Economic History of Europe According to Nigel Farage', so I'll keep it simple. All you need to know is that the main issues were low productivity (Greeks have an attitude to work that makes the concept of '*mañana*' seem like a state of urgency), government borrowing that spiralled out of control faster than Zorba's dance, interest rates higher that Demis Roussos's voice and the same attitude to paying taxes as they have to paying retail.

What will happen with the new left-wing led coalition government is anyone's guess. What I know for sure though, is that today's Greece is a country that's a mere shadow of its former self. It's ironic that a country that is considered to be the birthplace of western civilisation, which created fundamental new ideas in education, government, science, art, architecture and philosophy, has now almost been reduced to the status of 'developing nation'.

If Greece ever wrote its autobiography it would be called 'How The Mighty Have Fallen' or 'That Was Then, This is Now'. Of course, Greece would never write its own autobiography. Not because the concept of an entire sovereign state writing something down is an unfeasible, abstract one, but because nowadays it can't even afford biros or notepads.

10 Signs That the Greek Economy Has Been in Meltdown

1. There's been a huge influx of foreign visitors

Unfortunately for the economy these are not hoards of holidaymakers looking for sunshine, but financial journalists, political analysts and assorted nay-sayers arriving at Athens International Airport to report on the country's interminable slide into financial oblivion.

2. There's a huge shortage of magic markers and thick felt pens

Protesting locals have bought these up in their hundreds just so they can draw Hitler moustaches on placards of Angela Merkel.

3. ...and Prozac

How else do you think the population can deal with day-to-day life?

4. Signs outside shops that say, 'We accept hummus'

Many business owners have started looking for a currency with more long-term stability than the euro.

5. An air of despondency and gloom that sticks to the streets like the smell of rancid feta cheese

The general feeling of pessimism is not helped by news stories like a recent report on the world's strongest economies. Greece came out at number 214; there are only 196 countries.

6. **It's easy to get a restaurant table reservation**
   Brutal austerity measures mean that the locals can't afford to go out to eat (or indeed, eat).

7. **The concept of wealth has changed dramatically**
   These days, conspicuous wealth is anyone flaunting a takeaway latte or possessing matching shoes.

8. **Driving in Athens is a pleasure**
   The fact that there are few cars in Athens should not be seen as a progressive environmental measure but just that locals can no longer afford to run cars (many experience extreme financial hardship just filling up the windscreen washer bottle.)

9. **The locals look reflective and studious**
   Unlike their ancestors they're not getting to grips with trigonometry and algebra; they're calculating how they're going to survive on a 30 per cent pay cut and no pension.

10. **...and they're very philosophical**
   These days though it's less about Plato's belief in the immortality of the soul, and more about wondering how they're going to get through the rest of the week.

Lies, Damn Lies and the EU

'*Countries joining the European Union are akin to middle-aged couples with failing marriages meeting in a darkened hotel room in Brussels for a group grope.*'
– ANONYMOUS

The European Union

Think of it as one of the Sirens of Greek mythology; using its sweet song on member countries, seducing them with promises of prosperity and political stability, but instead luring them on to the rocks of financial calamity and brutal federalism.

Starting with the Treaty of Rome and continuing through its various insidious incarnations, the EU has systematically eradicated member countries' sovereignty in order to create a single entity – one where an unelected über civil service dictates and controls the lives of every European citizen. This is an ambition that goes by a number of names including a 'Federal Europe', the 'United States of Europe' or 'Hitler's wet dream'.

In 1973 the UK joined the EU (then called the EEC) in order to ensure a free trade agreement with member states. In return it's given up a significant part of its autonomy to a bullying, deceitful, evil, despotic bureaucracy.

Faust made a better deal.

FAQs About the EU

I've heard that the EU engenders peace and harmony within member states

That's true if your idea of peace and harmony is represented by massive unrest and widespread violent protests from Lisbon to Nicosia due to high inflation, tax rises, job cuts, loss of pensions and meteoric rises in unemployment.

I've also heard that EU officials are dynamic and progressive policy makers

Look. Where are you getting your information from? Brussels bureaucrats redefine the words 'faceless' and 'bland'. If they were an ice cream flavour they wouldn't even be vanilla; instead they'd be the scoop festering at the bottom of the bowl of dirty, lukewarm water.

Isn't the EU just concerned with legislation that's essential for the wellbeing of European citizens?

Well on the one hand, the EU has passed laws that grant unwarranted human rights to convicted terrorists; on the other, it has issued detailed legislation that defines the acceptable curvature of bananas and cucumbers. Make up your own mind.

Wasn't the EU founded on the principles of open justice, fairness and equality?

Put it this way, in the UK you're considered innocent until proven guilty. This principle is abhorrent to EU lawmakers whose European Arrest Warrant means that you can be accused of a crime in one country and extradited without trial, purely on the basis of someone filling in forms correctly. As Ian Hislop, editor of *Private Eye*, once famously said, 'If that's justice, then I'm a banana' (although under EU law, not a very curved one).

When it comes to the running of government, doesn't a centralised EU Commission mean huge savings?

It does, if by 'huge savings' you mean 'colossal waste'. For starters, it spends over €5 million each year on chauffeured limousines to transport MEPs like me around Strasbourg or Brussels. Then there's the 20 official recognised languages and 380 language permutations within the EU which means it spends more than €1 billion each year on translation and interpretation services.

And that's 'squandering tax payers' money' in any language.

I read that all EU funded projects are carefully vetted in order to provide the best value for European citizens
You're really reading the wrong sources aren't you? Recent EU handouts included £660,000 to Brazil to fund a project concerned with the 'social integration of women living in fishing villages', £240,000 to Russia for an arts project in St Petersburg entitled 'Listening to Architecture', almost £50,000 to create a 'European hip-hop laboratory' in Lyon, France… and don't forget £1.8 million spent on offices and a luxury hotel and apartment complex to house EU officials in that frantic hub of European political action: Barbados.

But at the end of the day the EU is democratic, right?
Mmmmmm. If you subscribe to the Pol Pot or Genghis Khan school of democracy then you're absolutely correct. Members of the European Commission are not elected by the voting public yet they can introduce policies that individual national governments are legally bound to undertake even though they weren't part of their own election manifesto. Even Kim Jong-un would feel uncomfortable wielding that degree of power.

Don't most people have a deep-rooted interest in European politics and want to actively engage with EU decision makers?
In a word, 'no'. In four words, 'Don't be bloody stupid.' Can you name more than one MEP (apart from me)? Have you ever voted in a European election? Do you understand the

significance of the Treaty of Paris, the Treaty of Rome or the Maastricht Treaty? Do you know the difference between the European Parliament, the European Council and the European Commission? Can you name the country that currently holds the EU presidency? Do you give a rat's arse?

Doesn't a fixed exchange system, common monetary policy and price transparency make the euro a robust and appropriate currency?
Go away.

Exercise the UKIP Way

Look, I am not saying at all that I necessarily agree with all of their policies, but the Nazis firmly believed that physical exercise greatly improved the morale and productivity of the workers – and I do too. People often say to me, 'Nigel, as a busy MEP, how on earth do you find time to stay in shape?' Well I get all the exercise I need by jumping to conclusions, running down the Coalition, side-stepping major issues and lifting pints. Of course, I jest! Actually, I keep fit by doing lots of walking around Brussels and Strasbourg… sometimes for hours on end, as there's very little of any interest in these godforsaken cities to stop at or visit.

What I don't understand, though, is why people waste hundreds of pounds each year going to gyms. Back in my day, keeping fit was simple. You had medicine balls, chest expanders and pommel horses. You couldn't go wrong with a medicine ball (unless you got hit in the balls, of course).

Nowadays gyms are filled with pieces of equipment that no one really knows how to work and which look more at home in Guantanamo Bay than in a suburban health club. The other thing that's changed is that a whole new language was invented to make people believe that keeping fit is dynamic and sexy. Exercise became 'working out', changing rooms became 'locker rooms', and jumping up and down became 'aerobics'. What's more, it's now all about abs, sets, reps, quads, delts, crunches and lateral pull-downs… you need a dictionary just to get by.

And what's the point in exercising in front of a huge mirror? If I wanted to know how out of shape I was, I'd ask my wife.

12 Reasons Why I Won't Ever Belong to a Trendy Health Club

1. They smell of sweat and desperation…
2. …and have background music that makes it feel like you're in a Bulgarian disco.
3. You have to pay through the nose for this form of humiliation, and the bargain 'off peak' membership usually means you only have access between 10am and midday on a Monday.
4. Communal changing rooms; if I wanted to see other men naked I'd change my sexual orientation and hang around bars called Spartacus, Ramrod or the Toolbox.

5. Men who spend all their time in the free weights area are likely to be serial killers or sex pests.
6. All the equipment is covered by an invisible veneer of sticky perspiration.
7. The personal trainers look you up and down like you're an out-of-condition slob or a worthless piece of shit. Usually both.
8. Seeing well-defined muscles in the changing room does nothing to improve your sense of low self-esteem.
9. You can find yourself crouching down tying your shoelaces just inches from a naked man's penis.
10. Driving to the gym usually takes longer than working out.
11. Most of the equipment has a control panel so complicated it wouldn't look out of place on the bridge of a Klingon battle cruiser.
12. Walking and running are free.

Stress Your Way Thin

It's been scientifically proven that anxiety can cause weight loss. As a 'Big Picture' kind of guy I don't understand the detail and to be honest, don't really need to. It's something to so with metabolic energy and fat oxidation. I think. Or it may not be. Anyway, it doesn't really matter. What does matter is that without doing any physical exercise, just bring stressed can help you burn calories. It might be a few here and a few there but by the end of the week it all adds up. I know that after a stressful week at the EU Parliament fighting against the erosion of UK's sovereignty I can easily lose a few pounds.

That got me thinking… how we can get ourselves stressed out on purpose in order to lose weight? From extensive research (and no, I can't provide documentary proof) I've compiled the list below that shows what calories UKIP supporters can hope to lose in a number of different situations likely to lead to high anxiety.

STRESSFUL SITUATION A UKIP SUPPORTER MIGHT FIND THEMSELVES IN	CALORIES BURNED
Shouting at the TV or radio	22
Throwing something at the TV or radio	28
Writing letters of complaint about political bias to *Newsnight*	35
Watching Alan Carr on TV	17
Listening to rap music	34
Listening to any form of ethnic music like bouzouki, steel drums or pan pipes	32
Having to change money into euros before you go on holiday	23
Mentally converting euros to sterling when you're on holiday	29
Watching a foreign art house movie with subtitles	38
Seeing a photo of Angela Merkel	39
Just thinking about Jean-Claude Juncker	86
Having someone yodel within earshot	11
Watching *An Inconvenient Truth*	16

STRESSFUL SITUATION A UKIP SUPPORTER MIGHT FIND THEMSELVES IN	CALORIES BURNED
Having to consider the other side of a rational argument	29
Being stuck behind a meandering procession of spotty foreign students with backpacks the size of Andorra	37
Being unable to overtake a bunch of wobbling lycra-clad idiot cyclists who change their speed with even more unpredictability than the Chaos Theory	62
Having to work out a time that's been stated in the 24-hour clock	21
Looking at a banana and thinking about whether or not it meets EU regulations about curvature	8
Being stopped in the street and asked to donate money for some foreign famine/natural disaster/ civil war, etc., etc.	22
Trying to make yourself understood to a bloke in a Mumbai call centre who tells you his name is Gary	34
Driving past a wind farm	13
Receiving an invitation to a same-sex wedding	29
Attending a same-sex wedding	72
Attending a same-sex wedding as the best man/woman	110
Being late for a gig by a progressive rock band or Phil Collins	31
Finding the newsagent has run out of copies of the *Daily Express*	94

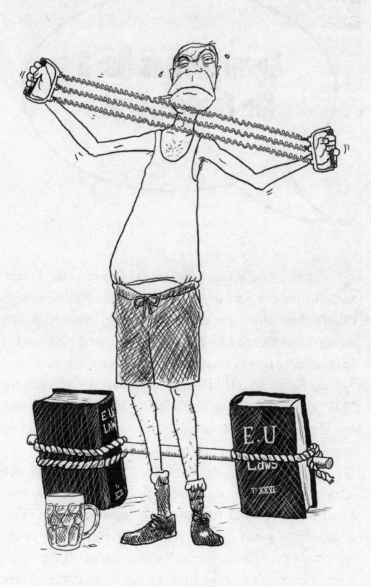

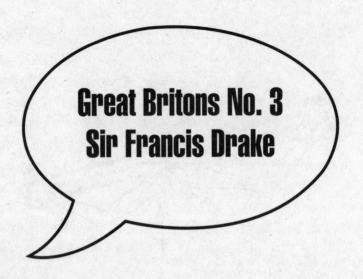

Great Britons No. 3
Sir Francis Drake

Sir Francis Drake was a thoroughly decent bloke. I think of him as a sort of Elizabethan Leslie Philips, though I don't think there are any contemporary records of him saying, 'Ding Dong.' Anyway, the English loved him and the Spanish hated him... what better reputation can a man have?

Their King Philip II offered a reward of 20,000 ducats for Drake's head, a currency that was the forerunner of the euro and therefore worth about £32.50, so no one could be arsed to risk their life and capture him.

Early in his career Drake sailed to the Americas and also made two voyages to the West Indies. Not much is known about these trips but they probably involved cricket. That or slavery. Anyway, in 1577 Queen Elizabeth I sent Drake off to fight the Spanish on the Pacific coast of the Americas; it was a journey that took him and his flagship, the Golden

Hind, all the way round the world. On the way he captured loads of Spanish treasure ships and, doing the decent thing, once he'd offloaded their gold he'd send their crew on their way with a letter of safe conduct. What a gent! He arrived triumphantly back in Plymouth in 1580 with a ship filled with gold, jewels and spices, heralded as the first Englishman to circumnavigate the world. He was knighted the following year, with Elizabeth getting a French diplomat to perform the ceremony for this British hero. Good call, queenie! Talk about rubbing Frenchie's nose in it!

Drake did lots of other heroic stuff after that, mainly involving attacking Spanish naval and merchant ships. God, he must have really hated those dagos. This obviously really pissed off King Philip II, who planned an invasion of England in 1588, sending his Armada up the English Channel. Like all Englishmen Drake was cool, calm and collected and he finished a game of bowls (or it might have been cricket, reports are sketchy) before he successfully attacked the fleet, causing them to break formation and show their true colours (the wide yellow band in the Spanish flag represents their cowardice).

After this victory he fought against the Spanish in South America but sadly, in 1596, he died from dysentery off Panama. He was just 55. Some people think that he might have survived if he'd had quicker treatment from the cash-strapped NHS. The fact UKIP wants to protect frontline health services from cuts means his death won't have been in vain.

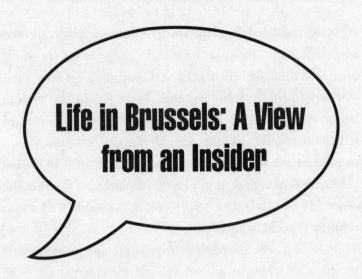

Life in Brussels: A View from an Insider

Since I spend a lot of my time at the European Parliament fighting for the rights of honest hard-working British citizens, I think I can speak with some authority about Brussels. Capital cities are meant to be exciting, dynamic and vibrant: a showcase of a nation's history and its contribution to the fields of art and culture. Given Belgium's reputation as a place to go through rather than to, it shouldn't surprise you then to learn that Brussels is best known as being the unofficial capital of the EU, the world's biggest, most tiresome, faceless and loathsome bureaucracy.

When I'm not opposing the encroachment of the European Union into British public life I relax by taking a stroll round the city, sampling Belgian bars and Belgian beers and taking in some of the sights. This is just another way I'm working for my constituents; I've visited these godforsaken places so they won't have to…

Local Attractions to Avoid

The Manneken Pis fountain
London has its 170-foot Nelson's Column, New York has its 150-foot Statue of Liberty, Rio de Janeiro has its 98-foot tall Christ the Redeemer. Even Baghdad had that 40-foot statue of Saddam Hussein before it was pulled over. The most famous statue in Brussels is that two-foot bronze sculpture of a boy urinating.

It represents what most visitors feel about this dismal city.

The Parliamentarium
The European Parliament calls this a visitors' centre. If you change the word 'visitors' for 'propaganda' then you'd be more accurate. As such it was designed to educate children and adults 'about the institution that represents them'. Again, if you change the word 'educate' for 'brainwash', then you'd have a better idea of what goes on here. However, despite having an obscenely high EU-funded promotional budget, the Parliamentarium fails dismally at being anywhere near interesting. The best come-ons it can offer (and I'm quoting the actual attraction here) are: 'The history of European integration using 150 iconic images and historic documents', a video titled 'United in Diversity', and an 'innovative and entertaining role-play game to see what it's

like to be an MEP'. Look, I am one and, to be frank, it's not that exciting.

Although admission to the Parliamentarium is free, you'll still feel short-changed.

Atomium

This structure of nine large interconnected chrome balls is often seen in the background of 1960s and 1970s budget sci-fi films to give an impression of some future Utopia. The Belgians are not known for their sense of irony but should be applauded in this instance. But don't be fooled; these aren't just any nine large interconnected chrome balls; they represent a unit cell of an iron crystal magnified 165 million times. If you want to pay to venture inside this relic from the 1958 World's Fair you'll see various exhibits, but absolutely nothing that will hold your interest. Reactions to this landmark from visitors vary from 'exceedingly disappointing' to 'Why?'

Mini-Europe

If there's one thing worse than the concept of a united Europe, it's the concept of a united Europe on a miniature scale. And this is it. If you thought model villages were a quaint concept that went out of fashion in the 1950s, you were wrong. Situated next to the Atomium, the Mini-Europe attraction promotes itself as 'the only park where you can have a whistle-stop tour around Europe in a few short hours'. 'A few short hours?' Believe me, no time spent here, even if it's even a cursory glance, will seem 'short'. 350 buildings in 80 cities are represented but in a blatant case of marginalisation, you won't be at all surprised to know that Belgium and the Netherlands each have 10 exhibits while France and Germany feature eight. The UK has only six, just one more than Portugal... and who can name one famous Portuguese building?

Not surprisingly, at the end of the visit you're subjected to another turgid piece of EU propaganda, the Spirit of Europe, 'an interactive overview of the European Union in the form of multimedia games'. NB The phrase 'multimedia games' implies some sort of fun. Don't be misled.

Tintin murals
Great Britain gave the world Chaucer, Shakespeare, Dickens, Wordsworth, Tennyson, Hardy, Blake, the Brontës, Tolkien, Austen, Keats, Coleridge, Eliot, Carroll, Wilde, Du Maurier, Orwell and Rowling. Belgium's contribution to literature is Hergé, creator of Tintin. Walking around Brussels you'll see numerous large-scale murals on the sides of buildings depicting scenes from his adventures. If you've never read Tintin, count yourself lucky. The books are as dull and long-winded as Brussels' bureaucracy.

Museums, various
Museums can often be a window into the soul of a country, let alone somewhere to get out of the rain. Like much of the rest of the city, Brussels' museums are equally lacklustre and

uninspiring, with whole buildings dedicated to celebrating the history of the Belgian police force, the National Bank, Art Deco ceramic clocks and also lace (yes really).

Useful Phrases to Use When You're in Brussels

Belgium has three official languages – Dutch, French and German – which means there's three times the likelihood of not being understood. Although 60 per cent of the population speak Dutch, French is the preferred language. This means that visitors have to remember crucial differences. For instance, a sandwich is masculine, despite having no penis.

I'd like to book an earlier return flight. Your capital city has sucked all the happiness out of me.
Je aimerais réserver un vol de retour plus tôt. Votre capitale a sucé tout le bonheur hors de moi.

Please stop bothering me. I'm trying to have a quiet drink and don't want to discuss the Treaty of Lisbon or the Central Bank.
Se il vous plaît arrêter de me déranger. Je essaie de prendre un verre tranquillement et je ne veux pas discuter du traité de Lisbonne ou la Banque centrale.

I apologise for laughing, but how can I take you seriously when your country's major contribution to modern culture is The Smurfs?

Je me excuse pour rire, mais comment puis-je vous prends au sérieux quand contribution majeure de votre pays à la culture moderne est Les Schtroumpfs?

---

4 REASONS YOU KNOW YOU'RE IN BELGIUM

1 Everyone loves beer.
'A Belgian goes into a bar' is not a joke. It's a continual occurrence.

2 Locals confuse 'picturesque' with 'lacklustre'.
Similarly, they confuse the phrase 'hidden gem' with 'nothing to do here'.

3 You're perpetually wet. And when you're not wet, you're damp.
Belgium enjoys an average of 200 days of rain per year which means it's either raining, about to rain, or has just finished raining.

4 You'll get French fries served with absolutely everything
The Belgians claim they invented French fries and take every opportunity to ram this fact – and the food – down your throat. There's even a whole museum dedicated to French fries in Bruges. And I'm not joking.

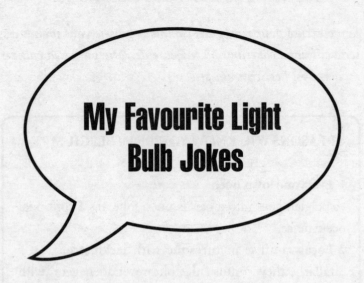

My Favourite Light Bulb Jokes

Given our calibre of candidates and type of grass roots supporters I can't understand why most of the time people are laughing *at* UKIP. In this instance, however, it's a chance to laugh with us:

Q: How many Somalians does it take to change a light bulb?
A: Four. One to change it and three to squabble over who gets to eat the packaging.

Q: How many schizophrenics does it take to change a light bulb?
A: Well, he thinks it's four but as we all know, it's only him.

Q: How many Nigerians does it take to change a light bulb?

158

A: Two: one to do it, and one to send an email saying that you've inherited $12 million in the will of an obscure relative – and could you send details of your passport and driving license in order to be eligible for your payout?

Q: How many inner city kids does it take to change a light bulb?

A: Five: two to rob the off licence to get money for the bulb, one to drive the getaway car, one to screw it in, and one to hold his crack pipe while he does it.

Q: How many Tory MPs does it take to change a light bulb?

A: Two: one to screw it in and the other to hang himself accidentally from the flex performing a strange sexual act involving a plastic bag and a ripe citrus fruit.

Q: How many social workers does it take to change a light bulb?

A: Five: one to remove the bulb from the socket and take it away without checking whether or not there was actually anything wrong with it; one to accuse its owners of mistreating it; one to find somewhere else to screw it in for the next six months; one to refuse the previous owner access to their old bulb; and one to eventually bring it back and say it was all done with the light bulb's best interests at heart.

Q: How many Germans does it take to change a light bulb?

A: 25,001. One to give the order that the bulb should be changed and 25,000 to say they were just following orders.

Q: How many dwarves does it take to change a light bulb?
A: Three.

Q: How many members of Amnesty International does it take to change a light bulb?
A: Two. One to change it, and one to stand on the street corner handing out leaflets looking earnest, and telling people how oppressed the socket is.

Q: How many gay men does it take to change a light bulb?
A: Three: one to change the bulb, and two to shriek, 'Fabulous!'

Q: How many heterosexual males does it take to change a light bulb in San Francisco?
A: Both of them.

Q: How many lesbians does it take to change a light bulb?
A: Four: one to do it and three to make a video documentary about it for Channel 4.

Q. How many women with PMS does it take to change a light bulb?
A. Three. Why three? IT JUST DOES, OK!!!!!!!!!!!!!!

Q: How many travellers does it take to change a light bulb?

A: One, but when they've gone you'll find all the other light bulbs in your house are missing.

Q: How many bleeding heart liberals does it take to change a light bulb?

A: None. 'Why should we impose our values on the light bulb? If it wishes to be a light bulb of no light, we should respect its uniqueness and individuality.'

Q: How many feminists does it take to change a light bulb?

A: Ten: one to change it, and nine to form a support group.

Q: How many members of an ethnic minority does it take to change a light bulb?

A: None – but a hundred will march on the power company supported by their union and demand that it hires some ethnic minorities to do it.

Q: How many hard-working Bulgarians does it take to change a light bulb?

A: Both of them.

Are You Manly Enough for UKIP?

L ook, I'm as broadminded as the next man but the sort of men UKIP wants as its supporters are real men. You know the type.

The fact you're reading this book probably means you are one. I know I am, and so are my mates in the pub.

I'm talking about the sort of man who doesn't care that much about his appearance and who laughs more at jokes about women drivers and mothers-in-law than internet dating or online shopping. Now I know we can't turn back the clock to a time before sexual equality and drink driving laws, but that doesn't mean that we can't look back fondly to a time when men were men… and women were fillies, birds or crumpets.

So, if your bar talk is more about moisturisers and *Dancing on Ice* rather than the Premier League or re-runs of *The Professionals* then you might not be the right sort of man we want associated with our party.

If you know what I mean.

Are You a UKIP Real Man?

Take this self-assessment test:

1   **Complete this statement: 'I wish I had…'**
    A. Brad Pitt's wife
    B. Brad Pitt's money
    C. Brad Pitt

2   **How much did you pay for your last haircut?**
    A. Nothing. Did it myself
    B. £6 to £25
    C. What, including my highlights?

3   **How many musicals have you seen in the last twelve months?**
    A. None. But I'm waiting for the stage version of *Expendables III*
    B. One. But it was *The Book of Mormon* and I only saw it because I wanted to take the piss out of another religion
    C. More than one

4 **Which of these headlines would most catch your eye?**

A. *TOWIE* Stars in Hot Lesbian Fling!

B. Ferrari Berlinetta Smashes Nürburgring Speed Record!

C. Versace Unveils New Sandal Collection!

5 **What oil do you usually smell of?**

A. Do you want me to punch you?

B. Castrol GTX

C. Patchouli or sandalwood

6 **What's your drink of choice?**

A. Beer or lager

B. Any spirit

C. Anything that's served with either a miniature umbrella or a sparkler

7 **Which of these women would you most like to take to dinner?**

A. Shakira

B. Tulisa

C. Bette Midler

8 **Have you ever had your eyebrows shaped?**

A. You really want me to punch you, don't you?

B. Yes. But accidentally after I got glassed in a pub fight

C. Of course. I'm not a savage

9 My favourite TV show is

A. Anything with Bear Grylls

B. The Simpsons

C. Anything with the word 'Dancing' in its title

10 My favourite karaoke song is

A. 'Eye of the Tiger'

B. 'My Way'

C. 'It's Raining Men'

11 How much do you know about Cher?

A. One or two things

B. A few facts

C. Where do I start?!

12 What's your favourite weather phenomenon?

A. Dramatic twister

B. Thunder and lightning

C. Big white fluffy clouds

13 What greeting do you use with your mates?

A. 'Hello' or 'Hi'

B. Nod, grunt and a fist-bump

C. 'You look FAB-ulous!'

14 How many pairs of shoes do you own?

A. 2

B. 4

C. 2 pairs each season

15 **How would you most like to spend a Saturday afternoon if there was no sport on TV?**

A. Chopping wood

B. Tinkering with my car

C. Shopping

RESULTS: WHAT TYPE OF ALAN ARE YOU?

Mainly A's: Alan Shearer

Whorrrrrrr! You're obviously a real man brimming with testosterone. You're someone who's able to keep his head above the tide of political correctness and male moisturiser. I welcome you and your sensibilities to the party with open arms (but in a very manly way).

Mainly B's: Alan Rickman

Wh-hey! A man's man and a regular bloke who takes no prisoners (except that, when Alan Rickman played Hans Gruber in *Die Hard*, he *did* take prisoners. I knew that).

Mainly C's: Alan Carr

Hmmmm. To be honest I'm not sure if you're the sort of type we really want to be associated with UKIP. The fight for UK sovereignty might not be your particular bent. Have you thought about a career as an interior designer, a hair stylist or a theatrical dresser?

How Can Good Manners Be So Foreign?

'An Englishman, even if he is alone,
forms an orderly queue of one.'
– GEORGE MIKES

Author Georges Duhamel stated, 'Courtesy is not dead. It has merely taken refuge in Great Britain.' He was French, so it was easy for him to recognise the appalling manners demonstrated by his fellow countrymen – and which sadly seem to be endemic among all foreigners.

Good manners are not just a sign of good breeding; they indicate respect and consideration for others, something that's deeply ingrained in Britain's DNA.

Unfortunately, other nations do not seem to hold good manners in the same high esteem as we do and it's quite common, when you're abroad, to find yourself dealing with locals who exude a combination of surliness and thinly veiled hostility.

In many cases it's difficult to tell if the person you're talking to is being exceptionally ill-mannered and rude – or is just being himself. Often there is no difference.

Closer co-operation with the EU won't just erode our state sovereignty and leave us open to an even greater influx of unwanted and unqualified spongers. It'll also bring us closer to European standards of behaviour and conduct…

Queuing

The concept of the queue is as alien to some foreigners as the concept of an honest day's work or having a sensible amount of body hair. It can drive someone from a civilised country like ours into blood-boiling fits of apoplexy. Have these savages somehow missed out on that basic childhood lesson of not cutting into line? Now you might expect people from the third world to ignore queuing protocols; when foreign aid workers drop off bags of rice or grain it's understandable that it's every man for himself in order to survive, but when you have to run the gauntlet just trying to buy toothpaste at a Naples convenience store it's totally unacceptable.

Surly Waiters

Bad manners among serving staff comes down to the fact that unlike Britain, most foreign waiters consider that their job is actually a profession. It's not. A profession involves years of intense training, continuous personal development and recognised qualifications. It does not involve a pad and pencil and the ability to push open a swing door without hitting someone the other side. The other problem is that as soon as foreign waiters see their job as a profession they decide that it's a profession that's beneath them. That's why every dish is served with a generous helping of arrogance and self-importance with a side helping of apathy.

Disinterested Sales Assistants

If England is a nation of shopkeepers, as Napoleon claimed, then France (along with all its European neighbours) is a nation of shopkeepers who have no concept of 'service with a smile'. This is because there is absolutely no comprehension of the word 'service', or the word 'smile.' To understand why, you need to appreciate that foreign shops operate with a different dynamic to what we're used to. In Britain the customer has money and the shop wants money – and will usually be very obliging in order to get that money.

Abroad the mentality is as follows: the customer has money, the shop has something the customer wants and therefore has the power – and they'll make damn sure you know. And although the concept of service with a smile may not exist abroad, there is one notion that definitely does: 'The customer is always wrong.'

Unhelpful Taxi Drivers

Give me a black cab driver anytime. By that I mean a driver of a black cab, not… actually it doesn't matter. Not only do they have an unbeatable knowledge of London but they're also intelligent and articulate on subjects like immigration, foreign workers, the UK economy and the draconian powers of the EU. It's actually amazing how much they have in common with UKIP policies. Anyway, I digress. Hail a cab anywhere else in the world and you'll find yourself being driven by a foreigner. That's not really surprising is it? But what I mean is that the foreigner won't be indigenous to the country you're visiting and will most probably be from Lagos or Marrakesh. That means he will have absolutely no idea of the local landmarks. Tivoli Gardens? Where? The Berlin Wall Museum? Never heard of it! The Vatican? Piss off, you're making that up! Not only that but their cabs will stink of goat curry (or similar) and they'll have world music blaring from their CD player so they can't hear you saying things like, 'That's the second time you've driven past the airport', or 'Why are we now in open countryside?'

With driving skills learned from watching the *Fast and the Furious* franchise and a blatant disregard of any navigational suggestions you offer, when you hail a foreign cab you end up taking two things: the longest route possible and your life in your hands.

A Complete Lack of Gratitude

One of the first phrases foreign language guides teach you to say is 'thank you'. Ironically these are the two words you're least likely to hear on your travels. Most foreigners seem to view uttering these words as a sign of huge weakness and will instead either refuse to say them, or begrudgingly replace them with a slight nod that's as imperceptible as their grasp of the fact that coming over here and cleaning car windscreens at traffic lights is not a real job.

UKIP and the Media

It's important to be aware that, just as in Iraq journalists and reporters were embedded in Fallujah, the British media is embedded in the establishment. This means they'll use every devious trick in the book to trip us up and make us look like intolerant, blinkered bigots. Sometimes, however, they don't actually have to try too hard.

Sadly, many UKIP candidates or supporters have a knack for inserting their feet when they open their mouths. Some of my colleagues' recent blunders have included claiming that gay marriage was responsible for flooding (look, I'm no Michael Fish so it would be wrong for me to comment on that one), mistaking Westminster Cathedral for a mosque (easily done in my view), or referring to women as sluts (a remark, for the record, that was taken completely out of context).

Even I was unfairly taken to task when I missed an important party event in Wales last December and blamed motorway congestion on the Coalition's open door immigration policy. I still stand by that remark and contest it was not a so-called gaffe. I got stuck behind a rusty R-reg Transit hogging the middle lane at 60 mph and it looked like it had a load of Polish plumbers in the back.

However, in order to convey our policies and views effectively and not come across as a bunch of fruitcakes it's vital that we watch our Ps and Qs when speaking in public (and by Ps and Qs I mean prejudices and quotas).

So, to help my colleagues become more media friendly, I've put together this handy guide.

Media FAQs

I have some very extreme views about race, gender and religion. Is that a bad thing?
Not necessarily, but for now keep these thoughts in your head. Don't write them down anywhere or say them out loud. They'll be plenty of time for that when we get elected.

So I can't say anything about using a giant catapult to send people back to Bongo Bongo land?
Er, no.

What about re-mastering the TV series Love Thy Neighbour *and issuing it free on BluRay?*

Haven't you listened to anything I've said?

What exactly can I say then?
Only things that are part of our published manifesto – as long as you convey these policies in exactly the same way as I've presented them.

What about if I want to use the manifesto as a sort of guide, but elaborate on it with my own ideas?
No.

Okay. How about paraphrasing it… adding a few extra bits here and there?
Look. For the last time, no! The language used has been carefully chosen to convey our thinking in a considered, intelligent way. One that shows we are a political force to be reckoned with and not a bunch of racist scaremongers with absolutely no idea how to run the economy.

All right. I think I've got it. Basically you're saying stick to the script.
Exactly!

Great. I'm off now. I'm being interviewed by the local paper about my idea to forcibly replace burqas with bikinis.
I give up.

The UKIP Guide to Acceptable Language

Language is constantly changing. It evolves and adapts to the needs of its users to accommodate new technologies, new experiences and new sensibilities. That's why there's been a need for new words like Walkman, laptop or blog – and why we now have to say feminist instead of lezzer.

If you're ever talking on behalf of UKIP it's vital to be aware of this ever-changing vocabulary.

THE WORD YOU REALLY WANT TO USE	THE WORD YOU HAVE TO USE
Tramp	Homeless person
Illegal immigrants	Immigrants
Parasitic underclass	Benefit claimants
Lazy arse	Motivationally dispossessed
Freeloading refugees	Displaced persons
Dolly bird	PA or Secretary
Foreign muck	Ethnic cuisine
Sponger's fund	Social Security
Batshit crazy	Mentally ill
Stupid	Intellectually challenged
Pikey	Traveller
Dole-office scroungers	Unemployed or Unwaged
Thick	Dyslexic
Cripples	Differently-abled/Physically challenged
Fairy / Poof	Homosexual
Bongo Bongo land	Africa

THE WORD YOU REALLY WANT TO USE	THE WORD YOU HAVE TO USE
Third-world shithole	Developing country
Poor	Economically marginalised
Fucking yuppies	Chattering classes
Blood suckers	Romanians
Shitty dump	Challenging neighbourhood
Shitty inner-city council estate	Community
Riff-raff	Working class
Four-eyed, two-faced lying bastard	Jean-Claude Juncker

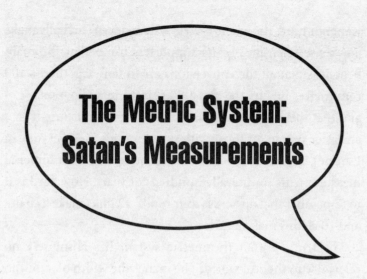

The Metric System: Satan's Measurements

If the EU had its way (or weigh... see what I did there), everything in Great Britain would be measured using the metric system. You'd be saying farewell to feet, goodbye to gallons, so long to stones and bye-bye to bushels. (Okay, I know we don't use bushels much these days, but I was struggling to find any alliteration for inches, ounces or pounds).

Losing imperial measurements would change our way of life overnight. Say you were on the phone chatting up a girl and you asked about her vital statistics. Suppose she said '91-61-86', how would you know what to say to her? 'Whorrrrrr!' or 'Don't go to the beach love, or Greenpeace will drag you back in the water.' This is just one example of how it would destroy our culture and heritage.

But apart from trying to foist something on us we neither

want nor need, the whole metric system doesn't actually make any sense scientifically. Its supporters claim that the main benefit is that all the conversions are in tens, e.g. there's 100 centimetres in a metre, and 1,000 grams in a kilogram etc. – and that this makes it an easier counting system. Sure it is… an easier system for those with simple minds (i.e. everyone in Europe). British brains have coped quite well with imperial measurements for literally hundreds of years. How hard is it to remember that an acre is four roods, 22 links make a chain, and 10 chains make a furlong?

The truth is that the metric system has absolutely no relevance to the real world. The inch is the width of a thumb so you've got something you can look at and understand right away. On the other hand one metre is equal to the distance that light travels in a vacuum in 1/299,792,458 of a second, while 1°C is equal to the fraction of 1/273.16 'of the thermodynamic temperature of the triple point of water.'

They're making it up as they go along!

The BOB System of Measurement

You're probably well aware that UKIP pledges to safeguard imperial weights and measurements but we're considering an alternative system too. It's a new measuring system that anyone can relate to, but which also has the added advantage of reminding foreigners of some of the symbols of our great nation. I'm going to call this the Best of Britain system (BOB) and the basics are as follows:

Length: measured in units of London Buses (LB), i.e. 36 feet 10 inches
Height: measured in units of Nelson's Column (NC), i.e. 170 feet
Area: measured in units of Football pitches (FP), i.e. 1.76 acres
Weight: measured in units of Victoria Beckham (VB), e.g. 110 lbs
Volume: measured in units of London Telephone Boxes (LTB), i.e. 24 sq ft
Speed: measured in units of Black Cabs (BC), i.e. 84 mph*

*top speed

Examples:

Under the proposed BOB system, say you wanted to express the weight of Angela Merkel, you'd say she was 1.90 Victoria Beckhams. Similarly, Jean-Claude Juncker's height would be 0.0293 of a Nelson's Column.

Simple.

Don't Let the EU Metricate the Film Industry!

Let the EU decide what units of measurement we use in the UK, and it won't be long before they make it mandatory for metric units to be used in every single walk of life. Take the film industry for example. You'll be on Netflix looking for the Tom Hanks classic *The Green Mile* and you'll see it renamed as 'The Green 1.609kms'. Similarly, you won't be able to watch Kevin Bacon in *Footloose*. He'll now be dancing his way through '0.3048m Loose'. And that's just the start…

Original title	What the EU will rename it as
My Left Foot	My Left 30.48cms
Fahrenheit 451	Celcius 232.778
Attack of the 50 foot Woman	Attack of the 15.24m Woman
8 Mile	12.875 Kilometres
The Beast from 20,000 Fathoms	The Beast From 36.576 Kilometres
Romancing the Stone	Romancing the 6.35 kg
Inch High Private Eye	2.54cms Private Eye
Happy Feet	Happy Metres
The Texas Chainsaw Massacre	The Texas 20.1168m Saw Massacre

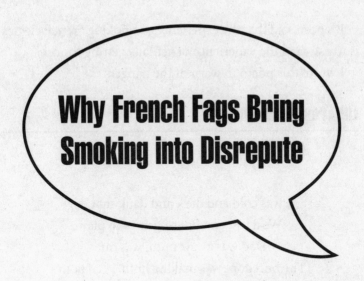

Why French Fags Bring Smoking into Disrepute

I love smoking. I love the taste and smell of tobacco. I love the fact that it's still considered an act of rebellion and defiance. I love the fact that it makes me look glamorous, sultry and sexy. But there's one thing I hate about smoking (apart from the fact that Government interference means that tax accounts for over 70 per cent of the price of a packet) and that's French cigarettes.

Smoking should be pleasurable. It shouldn't leave you with the impression that you've just spent time in a blazing tyre factory, or standing near one of those lorries that lays fresh tar on the roads. But that's exactly what it feels like smoking French fags or being near someone who is – a combination of a sharp, harsh flavour and nauseating acrid smoke that's been compared to burning flesh.

It's been said that the experience of smoking French ciggies is worse than the experience of actually getting cancer.

I wrote this poem to warn of the dangers.

The Frog in the Smog

A poem inspired by Dr. Seuss*

It was cold and dark and dank that day
We'd just run out of games to play
Dad was away; mum was out
The boredom was making both of us pout
Then all of sudden there was a loud rap
And again on the door, an equally loud tap

Bursting in came a striped-jerseyed frog
He entered the house in a pungent grey smog
He said, 'Bonjour, mes amis' to me and my brother
And then he asked, 'Where is your mother?'
'She is not here. She is out shopping'
'Bon! Bon!' he replied, constantly hopping
'We will have fun for the time she is out
We shall have fun, of that there's no doubt!'

'Who are you?' we asked, holding our noses
'There's a strange smell here; it's definitely not roses
That whiff, that pong, that very odd stench'
'Ah that,' he replied, 'It's because I am French

THE WORLD ACCORDING TO NIGEL FARAGE

I love to smoke. I love to puff
Sixty a day is hardly enough
The harsh, bitter fumes, I love them, monsieur!
Gauloises, Gitanes, and also Disque Bleu'

The smog it grew fast. The smog it grew thick
That stinkiest smell made us both feel so sick
It clung to the ceiling, it clung to the wall
Before very long it had filled up the hall
'To the lounge!' the frog cried, and hopped in there too
And as soon as he did, the smell followed through
It wasn't that long before all of the rooms
Were thoroughly, smellily filled up with fumes

Just then a hoot, a honk like no other
Someone was home. That someone was mother
What to do next? How to save face?
How to explain the smoking frog in this place?
We had to conceal him before mother caught on
But when we turned round, that frog, he had gone

Mother came in. Her face was like thunder
'I know what that smell is. I don't have to wonder!
You've both been smoking right behind my back'
And for that she delivered a most terrible whack

So the moral of this story is obviously clear
If you see a frog with a fag, don't let him come near

He'll stink up your house and cause you to choke
In no time at all, you'll probably croak
Don't let him come in. Don't take the chance
Slam the door and just say, 'Piss off to France!'

*Who wasn't a real doctor and anyway, if he was, he'd have taken early retirement because he'd be completely disillusioned by the way the NHS was being run by the Coalition, spending all his time form-filling and budgeting rather than caring for patients. I'm just saying.

5 Things That Really Wind Me Up About Germany

Hun, Fritz, Jerry, Kraut, Boche, Squarehead, Herman, Sausage Eater, Rhine Monkey… The Germans have one of the highest numbers of derogatory nicknames in the world – even beating the French (and that's quite an achievement).

Why then is there so much hostility towards the country? Well apart from starting two world wars and then becoming the economic powerhouse of Europe, Germany is mainly disliked due to two factors that directly affect visitors.

The first reason is the food. It's truly so bad that even Hitler was a vegetarian. The second is the language, which has been described as being extravagantly ugly; even a simple sentence sounds like someone using an in-flight sick bag.

And on the subject of language, only the Germans could have invented the concept of *schadenfreude*, the pleasure derived from the misfortunes of others.

And by 'others', it's anyone visiting Germany.

1. Germans have an anally-retentive approach to punctuality

I'm quite a stickler for detail and hate to be kept waiting but the Germans take it to the extreme. Saying to someone, 'I'll be there at about three' is as alien to most Germans as saying 'Tell me a joke', or 'Prepare me a meal that looks appetising'. A meticulous analysis of travel times and weather conditions enables Germans to pinpoint arrangements to precise times of the day like 09.27 or 16.53. And when they say 16.53 they get very disappointed if you arrive at 16.54.

2. Everyone loves techno music

Many people confuse techno with synth-pop or trance. Many more confuse it with music. This however hasn't dissuaded Germans however from adopting it and treating it with more fondness than even oompah bands. However if you're not a fan, it's hard to take a musical genre seriously when it relies on you popping pills or waving glow sticks to enhance your enjoyment. Techno lovers say there's more to it than clichéd synth sounds played over a mind-numbing repetitive drum machine beat. They are lying.

3. The choice of pornography

As you know I'm all for free speech and freedom of choice but even I think that the Germans take things a little too far when it comes to deciding what's acceptable in pornography.

Seeing sex acts between consenting heterosexual adults is one thing but looking at the top shelf and seeing magazines called *Donkey Liebe* ('Donkey Love'), *Scheiße Aktion* ('Poo Poo Action') or *Zwei Hunde und Eine Große Frau* ('Two Dogs and a Large Woman') make me feel a bit *unwohl* (queasy).

4. The food
Go into any restaurant and the waiter will say something like, 'Would you like some hasenklopse sauerbraten with your flädleschweiger?' How appetizing is that?

5. Mixed messages
It is truly puzzling to understand how a nation that introduced the philosophies of Nietzsche, Goethe and Kant to the world now holds David Hasselhoff in such high esteem.

---

3 Useful Phrases to Use In Germany

I didn't realise that you found punctuality such a turn-on.
Mir war nicht bewusst, dass Sie gefunden Pünktlichkeit wie ein Turn-on.

Please stop the yodelling and slapping dances. I have a severe headache.
Bitte beenden Sie das Jodeln und schlug Tänze. Ich habe eine starke Kopfschmerzen.

If your nation prides itself in its efficiency, why does
the Oktoberfest start in mid-September?
*Wenn Ihre Nation ist stolz auf seine Effizienz, warum das
Oktoberfest beginnen Mitte September?*

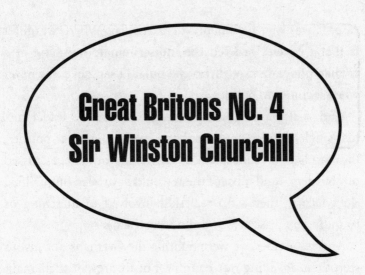

**Great Britons No. 4
Sir Winston Churchill**

A feature on Great Britons without mentioning Churchill would be like a feature on poor hygiene without including the French. I'm talking about Sir Winston Churchill here, not Churchill the dog from the insurance company, although saying that, he did give me a good price for comprehensive cover on my Ford Mondeo.

Anyway, I digress. Let's take a look at the life of this truly great leader. Okay, he might have a dodgy first name that's usually more commonly heard being said with a strong Jamaican accent, but he's one of the best blokes ever to have lived. The more I study him, the more I notice the amazing similarities between us. He loved a drink and a smoke, he didn't care who he upset, he was very unpopular with the Conservatives and the Establishment – and he worked tirelessly to keep foreigners out of Britain, although in his case, it was one nationality in particular. Where we differ is that I haven't ordered the indiscriminate bombing of a civilian population. Well, not yet but, as I say, never say never when it comes to politics.

And if it wasn't for his strong, charismatic leadership, his single-minded purpose and warmongering policies, thousands upon thousands of Germans would have crossed our borders – and most of them would have been unqualified (let's face it, there's no real skill involved in marching or rounding up prisoners and shooting them).

And remember, we were fighting the Germans not just to stop them invading our country, but to prevent their main objective – creating a united Europe; think of the Third Reich as a sort of forerunner of the Treaty of Rome.

It was Churchill's 'never surrender' attitude that galvanised the British people into action and gave them the wartime spirit that enabled them to see off the German threat. The consequences of Britain losing the war would have been catastrophic. By now we'd all be driving BMWs or Mercedes, using Braun shavers or electric toothbrushes, wearing Puma or Adidas trainers or Hugo Boss suits, taking Bayer pharmaceuticals and shopping in Aldi or Lidl. It hardly bears thinking about.

So, in closing, Churchill saw Britain having much more in common with the countries in the British Empire and the United States than mainland Europe. He polarised people but even his critics had to agree that quite simply, in times of national emergency, when the country was looking for direction and the British way of life and when all the values we held dear were under threat, he was the right man at the right time.

Do you believe in reincarnation?

I'm just saying.

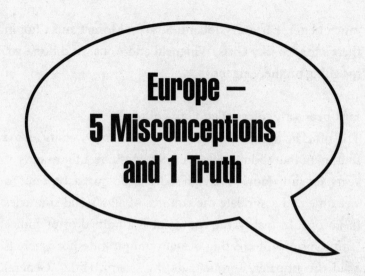

Europe – 5 Misconceptions and 1 Truth

Europhiles (a term that inspires the same level of abhorrence and loathing as the official term for kiddy fiddlers) always come up with the same tired old arguments as to why this particular continent leads the world in all sorts of things, from music and art to food and liberalism. In response I have two things to say to them: really? REALLY?

The Lies

Europe is responsible for some of the world's most creative artists

If I was writing this book in about 1865 that might have been true. In recent years however it's a whole other matter with Europe's contribution to world culture including The Smurfs, Asterix the Gaul and Topo Gigio. Music isn't that

193

much better. For every Johann Strauss, Mozart and Chopin there's the Cheeky Girls, Whigfield and Aqua. And don't get me going on the Vengaboys.

Europeans are tolerant and fair-minded

The official motto of the EU is 'United in Diversity'. It's a sentiment that should reflect a willingness, over thousands of years, for individual sovereign states to not just accept but to welcome and assimilate the cultures of all 50-odd countries in Europe. In reality, the continent is a hotbed of prejudice with a history of creating brutal tyrannical despots such as Vlad the Impaler, Torquemada, Mussolini, Hitler, General Franco, Slobodan Milošević and Angela Merkel.

Europeans are sexy

There's a common misconception that Europe is all about 'ooh-la-la' – conjuring up images of saucy French maids and smooth-chested Latino lovers whereas the reality of European 'sexiness' is obese, over-tanned businessmen wearing Speedos, and women with an aversion to shaving. And since when did pooing on someone become sexy, even in Germany? I must have missed that memo.

European cuisine is among the finest in the world

Supporters of continental cuisine point out just how creative and inventive European chefs have been over the centuries. This, of course, is correct. After all, who else would have had the imagination to think that cooking offal with two other types of offal was a good idea? Most exotic-sounding names on a foreign menu hide culinary abominations. For example, order *nozki* in Poland and you'll be served a plate of jellied pig trotters; select *kiaulės ausis* in Lithuania and you'll be able to tuck in to a selection of smoked pig's ears; or go for the delicacy *stracotto d'asino* in northern Italy and you'll end up with a bowl of donkey stew.

Europe offers a healthier life

According to a recent World Health Organisation study there are a number of small European countries that offer longer life expectancy than the UK and even the US. This might be statistically correct but I've included it as a lie as it's a fatuous argument in support of Europe. Why would you want to prolong your existence in Andorra and Luxembourg any more than you'd need? Switzerland too offers a higher life expectancy, but it's no coincidence that it also offers assisted suicide.

...And the Truth

Europe is a large melting pot of cultures

I can't disagree with this one, although I would point out that one consequence of a melting pot is that there will naturally be a scum on the surface. That's the Bulgarians.

Whatever Happened to Tunes You Could Whistle? My Guide to Music

Have you listened to the radio lately?

It's been said that the charts contain more evil than an al-Qaeda suggestion box.

In my day there were only a few different types of music. You either liked disco, soul, pop or rock. No one in their right mind liked country & western and even fewer liked jazz. Even Johnny hated it. Life was simpler then but now youth culture is so fragmented the whole music scene has gone bananas! In fact I think bananas might be an actual genre. Or it might be nu-bananas or bananas dubstep... Who knows? I read there are about 20 basic music genres and within these, 750 different sub-genres. That includes over 90 different types of hip hop and rap. Come on! How many different ways do you need to sing about the miserable reality of inner city life?

Now I'm as broadminded as the next man about music and have quite eclectic tastes. Listen to my iPod and you'd see what I mean. Put it on Shuffle and in the space of just a few minutes you could very well be enjoying the mellow tones of The Carpenters and Kenny G. But hold on to your hats! Next thing you know you're rocking out to Dire Straits, Genesis and REO Speedwagon!

However, there are some musical styles I just can't tolerate. Even the fact they exist at all offends me. I've listened to and have analysed the following genres so you don't have to:

Acid trance

If Derren Brown could hypnotise music (and he probably could; I've seen him live and he's really good), this is what you'd end up with: a series of electronic bleeps and tones that exist in a confused, puzzling trance-like state. A musical genre that's very popular in Belgium… and that really says it all.

Ambient music

You know that any genre that emphasises tone and atmosphere over traditional musical structure or rhythm is going to be rubbish. Since when did samples of whale song mixed with random electronic sound effects become known as music? I must have missed that memo.

Balearic beat

A style of electronic dance music that became a sub-culture in the British rave scene. This genre also became known as

'The sound of Ibiza', although this is not to be confused with a different 'sound of Ibiza' – the guttural vomiting outside one of the island's superclubs at 7am.

Death metal
Heavier than heavy metal and thrashier than thrash metal. Highly distorted guitars, abrupt tempo and key changes, grunting vocals and lyrics about satanism, vile hatred, massacres, being possessed, impaling, vivisection and torture. Not so much a style of music as your excuse to the court when you're charged with necrophilia.

Garage
Some people confuse 'garage' with the genres 'house' or 'dubstep'. Many more confuse it with the term 'music'.

Grunge
A combination of stripped down arrangements, distorted guitars and tormented, angst-ridden lyrics. One of the genre's biggest stars was Kurt Cobain of Nirvana who realised just how painfully depressing the music was and committed suicide.

Industrial metal
If I wanted to listen to the sounds of a hydraulic press, a jackhammer, or a milling machine I'd work in a foundry (well, I would if the Romanians hadn't taken all the jobs).

Nu metal

This has been described as heavy metal meets hip hop and grunge. As appealing as Ebola meets typhoid and cholera.

Rap

Whereas hip hop was upbeat and happy, and told people to get up and dance and have a good time, rap music takes itself very seriously. It's all about 'telling it like it is' and romanticising a depressive hardcore lifestyle. There are only 12 topics covered in rap songs: Glocks, Hoes, the Hood, Homies, Money, Cops, Sex, Drugs, Pimps, Prison, Bling and Gangstas. Not necessarily in that order.

Rap metal

Not so much a style of music; just two words joined together. Don't even bother.

Reggae

Reggae is the sound most associated with Jamaica, along with squad cars screeching to a halt and arresting another Yardie gang. Apart from their distinctive heavy backbeated rhythm, reggae songs can also be recognised by their lyrics which tend to be about three things: God (Jah), cannabis (ganja) and *Babylon 5* (Babylon). Two of the most authentic exponents of reggae were UB40 and The Police.

World music

The term 'music' is used very lightly here. I mean, it's hard to take any musical genre seriously when it involves the indigenous people of third world countries blowing nose flutes, banging pieces of pottery or playing a sort of xylophone made of hardened turtle penises. And who made oil drums a legitimate musical instrument? There are only two things you need to know about World Music. The first is that the Glitter Band and Adam Ant did primeval rhythms and multiple drums better, and the second is that when you've heard one song played on the pan pipes, you've heard them all. And don't ever get me started on Mongolian Throat Singing…

My Views On...
Modern Art

When the great British artist J. M. W. Turner painted *The Slave Ship* in 1840 he depicted a ship sailing through a tumultuous sea of churning water, leaving scattered human forms floating in its wake. Now I'm not using this painting to discuss the arguments in support of the slave trade (or even against it), but to point out that apart from being a fantastically atmospheric image, it's also extremely realistic.

If you gave a modern artist the same subject matter you'd probably end up with a wooden box containing sawdust, a length of vacuum cleaner hose and an old Wellington boot.

And that, in a nutshell, is the problem with modern art.

It's not so much a way of expressing yourself as a way to piss away a grant from the Arts Council. A grant that comes mainly from your taxes. I've been criticised for wanting to abolish the Department for Culture, Media and Sport, but can you blame me? When UKIP gets into power we'd still invest in art but I'd fill our galleries with works by real artists - not just by Turner, but also Blake, Constable, Landseer, Madox Brown, and even Rosetti and Millais (even though they don't sound British). These were people who knew how to paint; people who cared more about colour and composition than entertaining a gullible liberal elite.

I like to think I'm as broadminded as the next man but come on. If I displayed my unmade bed with dirty underwear and used condoms I'd be locked up in the loony-bin and my kids would be put on the 'at risk' list in the blink of an eye. I'm a genuine bloke; what you see is what you get (well, unless I'm concealing my true views of course) and I abhor affectation. Unfortunately the modern art world is overflowing with pretentiousness. Where else could you see a shopping basket painted gold containing a stuffed vole called 'The Physical Impossibility of Comfort Made Beautiful by the Inescapable Truth of the Virgin Mother Forever'? Or witness someone staring at a series of random pink blobs, who then says, without any hint of irony, 'It conjures up a self-conscious sexual paradigm and an oppressive male archetype.'

At the end of the day a bunch of coloured squiggles is still a bunch of coloured squiggles no matter how much you stare at them and scratch your chin – and a decapitated Barbie doll wrapped in barbed wire is not so much a comment on social inequality as the artist's silent cry for help.

And anyone knows that half a dead sheep is not a statement. It's a kebab.

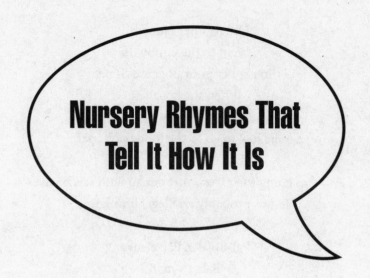

Nursery Rhymes That Tell It How It Is

Nursery rhymes need to be made more relevant.

I'm not talking about updating them for the poncey liberal elite who want to get your kids singing 'Baa Baa Rainbow Sheep', or 'Three Visually Impaired Mice', or any of that load of balls.

I'm talking about updating them so they reflect modern Britain – now a dysfunctional country thanks to the policies of Blair, Brown, Cameron and Clegg.

They had as much idea of what was good for Great Britain as Mother Goose.

It's raining,
It's pouring,
It's just the weather. It's got nothing to do with climate
change, you idiot

Old Mother Hubbard
Went to the cupboard
To get her poor doggie a bone,
When she got there
The cupboard was bare
So she had to go to the food bank again

As I was going to St Ives I met a man with seven wives
He was probably an illegal immigrant

Pat-a-cake, Pat-a-cake
Baker's man
Bake me a cake as fast as you can
Before the EU bans colourants and those really tasty
artificial sweeteners.

There was an old woman
Who lived in a shoe
She'd lost her job in the recession

Jack and Jill went up the hill
To fetch a pail of water
Jack fell down and broke his crown
And has to wait five months for an operation
thanks to Government
underfunding of the NHS

The Owl and the Pussycat went to sea
In a beautiful pea-green boat,
All they had was honey; they didn't bring money,
Not even a five pound note.
The Owl looked up to the stars above,
And sang to a small guitar,
We'll soon arrive in Dover where due to Britain's open-door
border policy
we'll soon be helping ourselves to Jobseeker's Allowance,
housing benefit and council tax benefit

The Grand old Duke of York
He had ten thousand men
But not anymore as the Government just announced
yet more jobs losses in the armed forces

Little Jack Horner
Sat in the corner
Eating his Christmas pie
Except we can't call it Christmas anymore in case it offends
non-Christians
so instead it'll be known as Winterval

London Bridge is falling down,
Falling down, falling down,
London Bridge is falling down,
I told you we shouldn't have hired those Polish builders

Ride a cock horse to Banbury Cross
Although the word 'cock' might be offensive to women
so instead we'd better just say horse

I'm a little teapot
Short and stout
Here is my handle
Here is my spout
I'm not really a teapot, I just think I am. But the
Conservatives'
Care in the Community policy has put
me back on the street
and I'll probably kill you in a random frenzied knife attack

Doctor Foster
Went to Gloucester
In a shower of rain
But now you'll have to go to your local A&E as your local
cash-strapped NHS trust can't fund
any more house calls

Georgie Porgie, pudding and pie
Kissed the girls and made them cry
They must have been lezzas

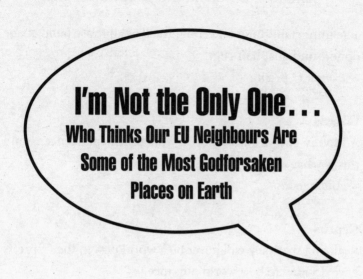

I'm Not the Only One...
Who Thinks Our EU Neighbours Are
Some of the Most Godforsaken
Places on Earth

Austria

No one clings to former glories as the Austrians do, and since these former glories include one of the most distasteful interludes in history, this is not their most attractive feature.

Bill Bryson

Belgium

Belgium is a nice place, though. It's the place people go to when they're on their way to another place, a place they're going to spend more time at. It's kind of the Jennifer Aniston of countries.

Craig Ferguson

Bulgaria

So what if you misplaced a little weapons-grade uranium?

The important thing is keeping track of all those hand-made doileys and goat hair rugs.

Conan O'Brien

Croatia

A bloody and brutal four-year War of Independence... and this is what we end up with?

Anonymous

Cyprus

Realizing that they will never be a world power, the Cypriots have decided to be a world nuisance.

George Mikes

Czech Republic

A land of disappointments.

Anonymous

Denmark

Beer is the Danish national drink and the Danish national weakness is another beer.

Clementine Paddleford

Estonia

The world does not understand Estonians, and Estonians do not understand the world...

Andrei Hvostov

Finland

Finland has long been a popular destination with travellers who enjoy the feeling of knowing that if their car breaks down, they could be eaten by wolves.

Dave Barry

France

The French are sawed-off sissies who eat snails and slugs and cheese that smells like people's feet. Utter cowards who force their own children to drink wine, they gibber like baboons even when you try to speak to them in their own wimpy language.

P. J. O'Rourke

Germany

The best thing you can say about Germany is that since 1990 there's only been one of them.

Anonymous

Greece

After shaking hands with a Greek, count your fingers.

Albanian saying

Hungary

Sins are born in Hungary.

Czech saying

Italy

Italy is not technically part of the Third World, but no one has told the Italians.

P. J. O'Rourke

Latvia

It's where Romanians go to feel better about themselves.

Anonymous

Lithuania

The Lithuanian is stupid like a pig but cunning like a serpent.

Polish saying

Luxembourg

On a clear day, from the terrace… you can't see Luxembourg at all. This is because a tree is in the way.

Alan Coren

Malta

There's one reason young Maltese men wear moustaches; it's so they can look like their mothers.

Anonymous

The Netherlands

Dutch is not so much a language as a disease of the throat.

Mark Twain

Poland

In the past few centuries, Poland has become known as 'the airplane lavatory of Europe' – dirty, subject to turbulence, and almost constantly occupied.

Chris Harris

Portugal

Take from a Spaniard all his good qualities, and there remains a Portuguese.

Spanish saying

Romania

Come see our museum of the Middle Ages. We call it 'Romania'.

Conan O'Brien

Slovakia

Potatoes are not food; Slovaks are not human beings.

Hungarian saying

Slovenia

Did a Slovenian feast take place here or did wild pigs run riot?

Anonymous

Spain

A wonderful country where there are only three things in excess: fleas, bed-bugs and Spaniards.

Victor Hugo

Sweden

Speculation is that the Swedes are slowly boring themselves to death. This is certainly the case if their cars and movies are any indication.

P. J .O'Rourke

Lie Back and Think of England – The UKIP Guide to Sex

Look, like most middle-aged British men I'm very self-conscious about writing about sex, let alone doing it. I know a lot more about the Euro Zone than any erogenous zone and have difficulty locating my car keys let alone any G-spot.

When I was growing up I learned everything I needed to about 'how's your father' from copies of *Spick and Span* and *Club International*. These days the Internet is probably the best teacher but stay away from some of those German websites. Call me old fashioned but I firmly believe excrement should be kept in the bathroom not the bedroom.

The one thing you'll learn from the Internet is how many different sexual positions there are. In my day there was just one but now it seems that the positions are only limited by your imagination and arthritis.

NB Because I'm so uptight writing about this subject, for the purpose of this feature, the word 'penis' will be replaced by the word 'Majority', while the word 'vagina' will be replaced by the phrase 'Ballot box'.

Sexual positions influenced by the EU

The Cameron/Merkel Congress

The man lies on his back with his arms at his side. The woman faces him and lowers her Ballot Box on to his Majority, holding it in a vice-like grip and enjoying the absolute power and control this position allows her. The man whimpers.

Brussels Style

The woman leans backwards against a wall with the man facing her. She sits in the man's cradled hands, her thighs gripping his waist and her arms around his neck. The woman prevents his Majority from entering her Ballot Box unless he can produce both a signed Sexual Consent Form 4435/665/h and a Contraception Affidavit 332/f, both of which have been completed with blue ink in block capitals throughout, accompanied by photocopies of his passport and countersigned by two independent witnesses.

Foreign Policy

The woman lies on her side. The man kneels behind her and grasps one of her ankles. He holds it aloft and tries to insert his Majority in her Ballot Box but it's flaccid. He tries

216

this several times but each time his Majority is more like a minority. The woman tilts her face towards him and laughs out loud at his impotency.

The Political Union
The man lies on his back with his legs apart and the woman kneels over his chest. The man twists his body to one side and raises one ankle. The woman arches her back. The man rolls over. The woman lays flat and lifts one leg. The man puts his hands on her shoulders. The woman grasps each of his ankles. The man grips the woman's waist between his thighs. The woman lowers herself on to his back. The man and woman realise they are incompatible and the whole experience has been a colossal waste of time. They separate.

Greek Style
The man positions himself behind the kneeling woman and thrusts his Majority energetically into her Ballot Box while shouting, 'I'm the European Central Bank. Take this, you bitch economy, take it!'

The Immigration Back Door
As above but the man inserts his Majority into the woman's bottom while shouting 'How's this for border control?' in a foreign language.

TWO SEX POSITIONS I RECOMMEND
FOR ALL MY CANDIDATES

Bloggy Fashion
The man updates his political blog in bed with his laptop resting on his chest. The woman faces the man, sitting astride his lap. His Majority is deep inside her Ballot Box. The man props the laptop lid against her breasts, and tells her not to rock forward and back too energetically because he's trying to delete that post suggesting that the Gideon Bible be replaced by *Mein Kampf*.

Reverse Bloggy Fashion
As above but the woman sits facing away from the man with the laptop lid resting against her lower back.

**UKIP Fairy Tales No.2
Snow White**

... After the huntsman had spared Snow White she wandered for ages in the forest until she came upon a charming cottage in a clearing. There was no one at home but she found seven small plates on the table neatly set out for dinner, and seven small beds upstairs. By this time she was cold, tired and hungry so she helped herself to some food and fell asleep in the bedroom.

That evening, when the owners of the cottage came home from work they were surprised to see that someone had not only entered their cottage, but had taken some food and drink from the table. But the biggest surprise was when they found Snow White asleep upstairs.

All this commotion awoke Snow White who sat up and rubbed her eyes.

'Who… who are you?' she said, nervously looking at the seven funny little men with beards who were staring back at her.

The first little man cleared his voice and spoke, introducing himself and his six companions.

'I'm Bureaucracy,' he said. 'One of the EU dwarfs.' Then, gesturing to his six companions, he introduced them all in turn.

'And this is Inefficiency, Incompetence, Intrusion, Confusion, Dispassion and Unaccountability… We've just got back from the European Parliament where we sit on various Working Group Steering Sub-Committees.'

Snow White beamed a beautiful smile. 'Can I stay with you? I'm hiding from my stepmother, the Wicked Queen.'

'Not unless you've got the form 45227/hl/331 Parts 1 and 2: a Permission To Lodge License,' Bureaucracy said.

'Oh,' said Snow White with surprise. 'I don't.'

The dwarfs all shook their little heads.

'But can I get one?' Snow White asked.

The dwarfs all laughed.

'Well, if you apply now it will take about ninety days,' said Inefficiency.

'Ninety-eight,' corrected Incompetence. 'And that's providing you're already in possession of a Woodland Transit Visa.'

'And while your application is processed there'll probably be a host of new EU prohibitions, restrictions, regulations and edicts, so you'll probably have to start your application all over again,' added Confusion.

'But I can't wait that long,' Snow White said, with a tremor in her voice. 'The Wicked Queen will be looking for me and I have nowhere to go.'

'Well that's not our problem,' shrugged Dispassion.

With that, the seven EU dwarfs manhandled Snow White out of their cottage and sent her on her way. She ran weeping into the dark interior of the forest.

A short while later there was another knock on the door. This time it was a huntsman holding a shiny new axe.

He bellowed in a deep voice: 'I'm looking for someone called Snow White. I've heard she has been in this area.'

The dwarfs looked at each other.

Then the huntsman handed them a piece of paper. 'I've got form 275/44/228/b, a Permission to Kill permit.'

Dispassion studied it for a moment.

'She went that way,' he indicated.

The End.

Spoken Like a True Patriot

Even though he was born in Hungary (a country best known for inventing the ballpoint pen, the Rubik's Cube, and red wine with the taste and consistency of cough medicine), author George Mikes (1912–87) had the good sense to settle in London and eventually become a British citizen. In 1946 he wrote:

'The world still consists of two clearly divided groups; the English and the foreigners. One group consists of less than 50 million people; the other consists of 3,950 million people. The latter group does not really count.'

Although Mikes wrote this nearly 70 years ago and the figures are way out of date, the sentiment still remains to this day – in fact, never has it been more relevant. But he wasn't alone in his thinking…

THE WORLD ACCORDING TO NIGEL FARAGE

Always remember that you are an Englishman and therefore
have drawn first prize in the lottery of life.
  Cecil Rhodes

Only two ways of doing things – the English and the other.
We'll not want the other here.
  William Donaldson

The English have an extraordinary ability for flying into a
great calm.
  Alexander Woolcroft

Other nations use 'force'; we Britons use 'might'.
  Evelyn Waugh*

Not to be English was for my family so terrible a handicap as
almost to place the sufferer in the permanent invalid class.
  Osbert Lancaster

If the French were really intelligent, they'd speak English.
  Wilfred Sheed

So little, England. Little music. Little art. Timid. Tasteful. Nice.
  Alan Bennett

The British are special. The world knows it. In our innermost
thoughts we know it. This is the greatest nation on earth.
  Tony Blair**

Because Great Britain has self-confidence, it doesn't need a monumental Olympics.

Ai Weiwei

Though the island of Great Britain exhibits but a small spot upon the map of the globe, it makes a splendid appearance in the history of mankind, and for a long space has been signally under the protection of God and a seat of peace, liberty and truth.

John Newton

Here's to Great Britain, the sun that gives light to all nations of the world.

Anonymous

---

*A brilliant author and journalist, even though he had a girl's name.

**A useless lying prime minister, but a good quote.

My Views On...
The British Empire

Atlases today have lost their way. Now they're full of maps showing human migration, urbanisation and even ice shelves. It was much simpler when I was at school. There was one map and half of it was covered in red. That was all you needed to see and it looked so much more attractive.

Losing the British Empire was tragic not just for the manufacturers of red printing ink but for everyone involved. Our great nation lost out on a ready supply of cheap labour and a ready supply of soldiers prepared to die for a motherland that they never knew nor cared about – but most of all, it lost out on the ability to exploit a wealth of natural resources.

This view however is not shared by those suffering from colonial guilt (which, for the record, like ME, ADHD or gluten intolerance, is just a made-up trendy condition). These whingers still resent our occupation. Talk about ungrateful! Those under British rule never had it so good. Sure, we exploited their mineral wealth and crops but look what we gave them in return; cricket, red tape, polo, picnics and jobs as servants. Not only that, but Empire building was an ancient custom practised by the Romans, the Greeks and the Macedonians. Convention and heritage should be valued and preserved wherever possible and all Britain was doing was maintaining this proud tradition – and for that we should be thanked.

Anyway, at the end of the day those in India, Australia, Africa, and even Aden and British Guiana should be thankful that they ended up as part of our Empire and not anyone else's. French imperialists would have introduced them to boules, quiche and adultery, while the Germans... well the Germans would have just killed them.

And of course, without our Empire we'd never have been inspired to produce such critically-acclaimed films like *Gandhi*, *Zulu*, *Lawrence of Arabia* or *Carry On Up the Khyber*.

Wind Farms: Don't Believe the Spin

As one of the last bastions of old-fashioned Englishness, we need to preserve the customs and traditions of the countryside. And by that, I mean a countryside that's exactly like the one portrayed in that other bastion of old-fashioned Englishness, *Midsomer Murders* (well, apart from the murders part).

There's something very comforting about living in such a middle-class, intolerant community, but nowadays there's a real threat to this rural idyll: one that's ruining the unspoilt countryside – and I don't mean travellers.

I'm talking about wind farms: less of a renewable green energy source and more of a way for the EU and our government to offer landowners massive subsidies to provide one of the most inefficient ways of generating electricity.

I'm so incensed by the sight of these monstrous turbines obliterating the horizon that I was inspired to put pen to paper...

Windmills

(Inspired by that great British poet William Wordsworth)

I wandered lonely as a cloud
That floats on high o'er dales and hills
There before me, was not a crowd
Of bright and golden daffodils
Instead across the whole wide vale
A host, of spinning silver sails

Hundreds I saw there, at first glance
Reaching up into the sky
Whirling and twirling in sprightly dance
Symbols of a great Green lie
An energy source so inefficient
Providing power that's intermittent

We were duped; we were tricked and deceived
By this blight affecting England's fields
Many are the reasons to be aggrieved
High subsidies; low power yields
That Climate Change Act; such a farce
Like a bunch of daffs; stick it up your arse.

5 Things That Really Wind Me Up About Italy

Michelangelo, Gucci, spaghetti carbonara, the Cosa Nostra...there are few places where art, fashion, carbohydrates and organized crime intermingle so effortlessly as in Italy. The Italians have a phrase, 'la dolce vita,' which means 'the sweet life': a life of pleasures and indulgences. Sure, on the face of it, Italy *does* seem to have everything; a benign climate, a host of cultural treasures, well-dressed criminals, an edible national cuisine plus a reputation as a country that's stylish, elegant and chic.

However, strip off Italy's stylish clothes and you'll see a country with a €2.1 trillion government debt that's slipping into economic turmoil quicker than a Naples pickpocket removing your wallet.

1. Everyone judges you

Walk down any street (or *strada* as they call them) in an Italian city and all eyes will be on you. All the locals will be checking you out, not because they think they recognize you or because you look cool or sexy. They're looking at what you're wearing. Brought up in a culture where's there's only two seasons (Spring/Summer and Autumn/Winter) and where a baby's first words include *doppio ventilato* (double vented), everyone is ultra-conscious about appearances. They call themselves fashionistas. You'll call them shallow twots.

2. Italians actually believe they can multi-task

Italians are proud of the achievements of their ancient Empire, the desirability of their sports cars and their ability to multi-task. Two of these aspects of Italian life are justified. Unfortunately, if you're a pedestrian there, multi-tasking is an unwelcome practice; nearly all Italian motorists think nothing of driving while reading a map, reading the paper, shaving, applying make-up, lighting a cigarette, drinking coffee, turning to speak to the passengers in the back and cursing the mothers or sisters of fellow motorists – and they carry out many of these acts simultaneously.

3. Italians are such hypocrites

I wish my PR machine was as good as the Italians. Mention Italy and most people think of these glamorous associations: Ferrari, Maserati, Gucci, Prada, Bulgari, Armani... the list of exclusive brands is endless (well, until you get down to

Zanussi and Nutella). Scratch the surface though, and you'll find a country that's as superficial as its lucrative fashion industry; one with perpetual political instability (more than 25 governments since 1980) and a reputation for lumbering bureaucracy and low productivity.

The persona Italy still keeps promoting to the world is Rudolph Valentino. The reality is that it's Joey Tribbiani from *Friends*.

4. It's like you're in a mime show

Whether it's a waiter, a policeman or your hotel receptionist, try and engage an Italian in conversation and you'll be at best puzzled, and at worst completely and utterly confused. They can have an entire conversation without actually speaking, relying instead entirely on eye movements, facial expressions and violent hand gestures. On some occasions it looks like they're conducting the Rome Philharmonic.

5. Tuscany: the Italian Islington

Tuscany is a region in central Italy, which is best known for its rustic landscapes, olive groves and vineyards. Its capital is Florence. Visit Tuscany in the summer and you'll hear high-pitched whining and feel irritable. This will not be due to mosquitoes, though, but an infestation of really annoying British middle-class families who look and sound exactly like David and Samantha Cameron.

3 Useful Phrases to Use in Italy

So that's the legendary Shroud of Turin. It looks like Billy Connolly to me.

Ecco, questo è il leggendario Sindone di Torino. Sembra che Billy Connolly a me.

You have a work ethic that makes the Spanish look like models of efficiency.

Si dispone di un etica del lavoro che rende l'aspetto spagnola come i modelli di efficienza.

I am very sorry. I didn't realise that the swarthy man I've just been talking to was actually your elderly mother.

Mi dispiace molto. Non mi rendevo conto che l'uomo dalla carnagione scura che ho appena parlato con era in realtà sua madre anziana.

**Great Britons No. 5
Phil Collins**

Not only a great bloke but an inspiration as well, I can really identify with Phil Collins.

Not because he's a short, bald, multi-millionaire, tax exile drummer. Like me, he's been constantly and usually unfairly vilified in the press, but has managed to rise above this. Phil and I have both had more than our fair share of criticism; it comes with the territory, whether you're a top musician or a top politician. The press regularly accuses me of being a closet racist or a Stalinist bully boy – and accuses Phil for being smug, boring and bland; an appraisal of his music in *The Guardian* once described Collins as 'un-stomachable' and his music as 'perfectly vacuous'. Sure those criticisms can hurt but Phil's professionalism and fortitude has meant he's maintained his dignity at all times – even after his track was used in that Cadbury's commercial, and he was described as a 'fat, bald, chocolate-eating bastard', or when Noel Gallagher said, 'Just because you sell lots of records, it doesn't mean to say you're any good. Look at Phil Collins'.

The fact that Phil has remained so stoic in the face of unprecedented vicious personal attacks like these has been a great influence on me. He took them on the chin and said to himself, 'I don't care what you say. I'm still going to make superficial songs for undiscriminating people.' Inspired by his resilience I follow his example, although obviously, in my case, I substitute the word 'policies' for 'songs'.

But it's not just Phil's tenacity and perseverance that's inspired me; some of his albums and singles have struck a real chord too. Take *Hello, I Must Be Going!*… if that's not a clarion call to leave the EU then I don't know what is. 'Another Day in Paradise' describes what I feel when I arrive back in England from dreary Brussels. 'Against All Odds' is about me trying to make a difference for this great country and, of course, 'In the Air Tonight' invokes the sense that victory will be ours come the election.

So, if you're reading this book, Phil, I'd just like to say once again that you're a top bloke whose attitude and actions have motivated and encouraged me in my own career. The only thing I find odd is that you've chosen to live in Switzerland.

Well, we can't all be perfect.

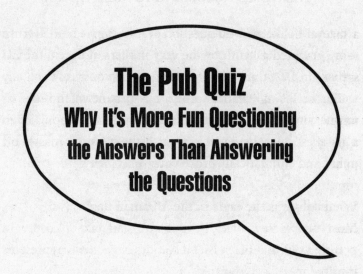

The Pub Quiz
Why It's More Fun Questioning the Answers Than Answering the Questions

Described* as a modern version of the Gladiatorial games, the Pub Quiz has become just as thrilling and awe-inspiring!

The amphitheatre has become the Red Lion, spears and tridents have been replaced by pens and answer sheets... but in every other respect, pub quizzes are just as big a spectacle as anything seen in the Colosseum.

Okay, we might not have combatants like Spartacus, Triumphus or Celadus the Thracian but their equivalents today are participants who are just as brave. I'm talking about teams like Smarty Pints, The Magnificent Bar Stewards and Les Quizarables.

And just like the Roman Games, a Pub Quiz is also a fight to the death (albeit a proverbial one). To the victor, the spoils (usually a £30 Pizza Express gift card)!

However if, like me, you question everything we hold as truth – or presented as truth by the very masters of deceit, the EU – then the best thing about entering a pub quiz isn't actually the prize. It's the chance to be a real pedant when it comes to querying the official answers. Here are some popular pub quiz questions where you can catch the question master off guard and emphatically prove your superiority:

What colour is the eagle in the Albanian flag?
Most people say 'black'… but you can take pleasure in pointing out that black isn't a colour… it actually represents the absence of a colour.

What is the most northerly point of mainland Britain?
Contrary to popular belief it's not John O'Groats. It's Dunnet Head.

What is the name of the statue with a bow in London's Piccadilly Circus?
Anyone that says Eros is an idiot! It's actually Anteros, the younger brother of Eros.

How many wives did Henry VIII have?
Just two I'm afraid… His marriages to Anne of Cleves, Anne Boleyn, Catherine of Aragon and Catherine Howard were annulled, which legally means they never took place.

How tall was Napoleon Bonaparte?
If you answer 'between 5'6" and 5'7"', you're correct! Most people will say 5'2" but this was his height in French feet, which were smaller than the standard (and far superior in all cases) English feet and inches.

Where do Newcastle United play?
The correct answer is 'St James' Park'. If anyone writes the answer 'St James Park' without the apostrophe, they need to be stripped of the point and publicly humiliated since this is the name of Exeter City's ground.

What is the Earth's tallest mountain?
No. It's not Everest. That's the world's highest mountain since height is measured from sea level to summit. The tallest mountain is Mauna Kea in Hawaii as measured from its base, which is on the floor of the Pacific, to its summit.

What was the middle name of the composer Mozart?
It's Wolfgang, idiot (or Wolfgangus, if you like). He was baptised as Johannes Chrysostomus Wolfgangus Theophilus Mozart.

*By me

My Views On...
The Homeless

When you come to think about it, the homeless are actually much better off than you or me. For a start they can sleep soundly at night, not having to think about negative equity, the shortfall of their endowment mortgage, a change in interest rates or repossession. Then there's the money they save and not just the mortgage. There's buildings and contents insurance that can cost a packet – and don't forget the council tax; they're exempt! How bloody lucky is that, saving a couple of grand a year? I wouldn't say no!

And apart from the money they save they don't have all the other hassles that homeowners have to put up with. I'm talking about things like neighbours who play drum and bass, or have babies who scream every half-hour from midnight to five in the morning, having to repaint the window frames, having to clear the doormat from double glazing circulars and Christian Aid charity envelopes, plus having inconsiderate sods park right across your driveway. And best of all, absolutely no worries about being burgled.

Lucky sods.

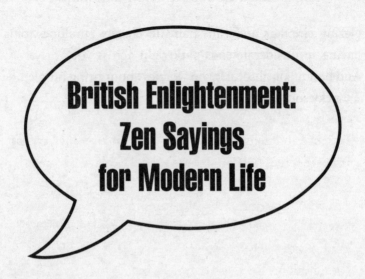

British Enlightenment: Zen Sayings for Modern Life

Zen wisdom is supposed to give us a special insight into compassion, love, peace, patience and humanity. If you ask me it's all a load of ancient foreign claptrap and, to be honest, I've received the same so-called 'enlightenment' on a tiny piece of paper that's come out of a Christmas cracker.

If we're going to learn anything from so-called Zen teachings then they have to be made relevant to life in modern Britain. As they say, 'If a UKIP candidate says something racist or sexist in a forest and no one is around to hear him, does he make a sound?'

Zen Sayings Reworked for UKIP Supporters

- The journey of a thousand miles begins with clinging to the chassis of a British lorry travelling from Dubrovnik.

- Watching Nick Clegg at the Lib. Dem. party conference: the sound of one hand clapping.
- Hide not your inner desires behind your outward expression. Easier said than done when you're wearing a burqa.
- Patience and determination can conquer all things, except when it comes to having to ring the BT call centre in Mumbai.
- Always be gracious, helpful and courteous to strangers. As long as they meet a points-based visa system and time-limited work permits.
- Do not follow the ideas of others, but learn to listen to the voice within yourself. Just don't tell anyone you can hear that voice.
- There is no such thing as a bad idea. Try telling that to Godfrey Bloom.
- The man who has everything needs just one thing: a sophisticated burglar alarm linked to his local police station.
- Music and rhythm nourish the secret places of the soul, unless you're listening to rap or hip hop.
- If you want one year of prosperity grow grain. If you want ten years of prosperity grow trees. If you want a lifetime of prosperity get an EU farming subsidy.
- Do not walk behind me, for I may not lead. Do not walk ahead of me, for I may not follow. Do not walk beside me for the path is narrow. In fact, just piss off and stop pestering me for a comment about one of our embarrassing candidates.

- There are many ways to effectively put your point of view to a *Guardian* journalist. None of them work.
- Walk as if you are kissing the earth with your feet. But speed up a bit when you're near an inner-city estate.
- Those who can find curiosity and delight in everything they see have probably never read our manifesto.
- Where there are dangers you will find fortitude. Where there are friends you will find kindness. Where there are idiot candidates, you will find my personal poll ratings plummeting.
- Even bad books are books and therefore sacred. Except for politicians' autobiographies.
- Time flows away like the water in a river, especially when you're waiting for an NHS appointment.
- Better to light a candle than curse the bloody foreign workmen outside your house who cut through a power cable.
- If your strength is small, don't carry heavy burdens. If your words are worthless, write for the *Daily Telegraph*.
- There are no facts, only interpretations. Which is why you should really believe our views on climate change.
- The journey is the reward. Unless the country's open-door immigration policy gets you stuck on the M4.
- Nothing is more dangerous than sincere ignorance and conscientious stupidity. The proof is watching *Big Brother* contestants.

Party Fundraising
It's a Piece of Cake!

When it comes to raising money for good causes you have to admire Macmillan. I'm talking about the charity, not the over-privileged post-war toff PM. Once upon a time cancer was a taboo subject. It was associated with heavy smokers, those who worked with asbestos or nuclear waste – or who lived near Hiroshima. We were all in denial about cancer; it was something just whispered about like male pattern baldness, erectile dysfunction or fancying Ed Miliband's wife.

Now we're much more open about it, with celebrities like Lance Armstrong, Angelina Jolie, Kylie Minogue and even Olivia Newton-John talking about fighting the disease. But if there's one thing more fashionable than having cancer, it's raising money to fight it.

I wanted to take a leaf out of Macmillan's book and, after discounting going on a fun run wearing a pink tutu, I decided UKIP should hold its own World's Biggest Coffee Morning. The challenge was making it different from the Macmillan fundraiser.

That's when I had my brainwave.

We'd ditch the cupcakes (or as they were known in my day before the politically correct brigade stuck their noses in, fairy cakes) and instead bake and sell a cake that the public firmly associated with UKIP.

The recipe's overleaf so get baking!

THE UKIP FRUIT CAKE

INGREDIENTS

As you know I'm not that good with detail,
so let's just say you need some dried
fruit, flour, eggs, sugar and treacle. Oh
yes, don't forget the brandy or sherry,
lemon juice, ground almonds, cherries
and probably baking powder if I'm not
mistaken. Did I mention brandy or sherry?
I might have. Anyway, there might be
some more stuff. I'm not really sure.

METHOD

All I know is that you mix stuff up, add things and put
the mixture in an oven. If you want my advice ask a
woman to do it. She'll know about baking cakes (they
always do).

UKIP Fairy Tales No. 3
The Three Little Pigs

… The next day, the Big Bad Wolf was walking along the road. He came to the house of straw that the first little pig had built. The wolf knocked on the door and said, 'Little pig, little pig. Let me come in!'

But there was no answer.

He knocked again, and this time shouted, 'Little pig, little pig. Let me come in!'

Still there was no answer.

'Mmmmm. That's odd,' he thought. Then he saw a fox coming towards him.

'Excuse me, Mister Fox,' the Big Bad Wolf said, 'But I was wondering where the little pig who lives here is. I want to huff and puff and blow his house down.'

'He's not here anymore,' said the fox. 'His company couldn't compete with cheap migrant labour from Eastern Europe and he lost his business. The bank took his home.'

'Oh,' said the Big Bad Wolf. 'In that case I'll visit the little pig with the straw house.'

'He's not there either,' explained the Fox. 'He was meant to have an operation but he was turned away twice because the hospital didn't have a bed. His health worsened and he died last week.'

'Oh,' said the Big Bad Wolf again. 'Then tell me, Mister Fox,' he said, 'What about the little pig with the house made of bricks. He's all right, isn't he?'

'Sadly, Big Bad Wolf, he is not,' the fox explained. 'He served in the military with distinction but had mental health problems when he returned to civilian life and slipped through the net of social services. He was seen last week sleeping rough.'

The Big Bad Wolf scratched his chinny-chin-chin.

'Wow,' he thought to himself. 'David Cameron and Nick Clegg have really made the country go to shit.'

The End.

My Views On...
Vegetarians and Vegans

I'm all for trying to educate our children to take care of their bodies and the importance of a healthy diet, but what kind of role models are we giving them if we tell them that eating meat is bad? Some of the world's most evil tyrants (not my words) were vegetarians. Most people know that in adult life Hitler refused to eat meat – so too did Genghis Khan – and he was said to have killed 1,748,000 people in a single hour.

Also, vegans aren't as peaceful as they'd like you to think. The murderous Pol Pot, leader of Cambodia's notorious Khmer Rouge was a vegan, as was animal rights activist and mass murderer Charles Manson. And aren't we meant to take guidance from the Bible? Remember Cain and Abel? They both brought offerings to God, who, the Bible says, had respect for Abel's carnivorous offering, but no respect for Cain's 'fruits of the ground'. Oh yes, and it was the vegetarian Cain who killed his brother.

The other argument put forward for a vegetarian diet is that it makes you smarter. Really? Well Albert Einstein became a vegetarian for the last year of his life and guess what? He didn't make any new discoveries – and he died! And don't get me bloody going on tofu or soya!

Beethoven: Why He's No Match for Phil Collins

Ludwig van Beethoven is often celebrated as one of the most famous and influential of all composers, but as a bit of a music expert who's studied the man and his music at length, I can categorically say that one of Europe's so-called best doesn't hold a light to the man who many say is his modern-day counterpart: Phil Collins.

20 Reasons Why Phil Collins Is So Much Better Than Beethoven

1. Beethoven only wrote nine symphonies. Phil Collins recorded 45 singles.
2. Beethoven never wrote lyrics as insightful as 'I feel so good if I just say the word Sussudio, just say the word, Oh Sussudio.'

3. Beethoven never won four Brit awards (not even in the International Male Solo Artist category).

4. Beethoven played the piano. Phil Collins plays the piano *and* drums.

5. Beethoven has been described as a crucial figure in the transition between the Classical and Romantic eras in Western music. Phil Collins has been described as a crucial figure in the transition between the Peter Gabriel era of Genesis and the band's more pop-oriented and commercially successful period.

6. Beethoven often played piano in the salons of the Vienna nobility. Phil Collins played at Live Aid. Twice.

7. Beethoven never starred in the flop film *Buster*.

8. The most maverick thing Beethoven did was compose a piece of music in the unusual key of C minor. In an episode of *Miami Vice*, Phil Collins played a shady drug dealing con man.

9. Beethoven never appeared on *Top of the Pops* alongside such greats as Bananarama, Toyah and Bucks Fizz.

10. Beethoven's dishevelled appearance once led him to be mistaken for a tramp. Phil Collins earned millions for writing a song about the homeless, 'Another Day in Paradise'.

11. None of Beethoven's compositions was played by a gorilla in a TV commercial to promote a chocolate bar.

12. Phil Collins inspired far more vitriolic hatred among critics than Beethoven.

13. Beethoven was completely unimaginative when it came

to naming his compositions, e.g. 'Symphony No.1', 'Symphony No.2', etc. But Phil Collins was much more creative with album titles like *Face Value* and *No Jacket Required*.

14. When Beethoven was 43 he was depressed and unproductive. When Phil Collins was 43 he embarked on his hugely successful 169-date *Both Sides of the World* Tour.

15. Proving the correlation between money and artistry, Beethoven was in financial trouble most of his life; yet Phil Collins is estimated to have a personal fortune of £115 million.

16. Beethoven never knocked Dead or Alive off the Number One spot.

17. Beethoven never married. Phil Collins has been divorced three times.

18. Phil Collins wasn't completely deaf.*

19. Phil is a far cooler name than Ludwig.

20. Beethoven was German. Phil Collins is British.

*Although it's been cruelly said that many of his concertgoers probably wish that they were.

5 Things That Really Wind Me Up About Spain

Look beyond a sovereign state set to follow Greece and Cyprus in an inevitable slide into a calamitous fiscal abyss, and you'll see a nation rich in history and tradition but with a fresh, modern outlook on life. A country with a kaleidoscope of landscapes, from beaches to sunburnt plains and mountain peaks. A country that combines technology and a very modern infrastructure with the highest levels of disorganisation, lethargy, incompetence and a questionable understanding of the word 'productivity'.

Yes, Spain is truly a land of contrasts; it's where an industrialised nation meets a banana republic.

1. The Spanish are so noisy
Most Spaniards confuse talking with shouting, a situation

exacerbated by the fact that they are incapable of having a conversation unless they are standing at least six feet apart, or more usually, on opposite sides of the road. At times this can give the impression that they are being aggressive. In many cases they're not; that couple who look like they're having a blazing stand-up row in the street are probably just discussing the weather.

2. Levels of bureaucracy that would astound even Kafka

If you're in Spain, pray to God that you never, ever have to deal with any government office. If you even manage to find one, government offices in Spain only open at certain times on certain days of the week and by the time you've reached the front of the serpentine queue it's highly likely that local regulations would have changed, so you'll have to go back and complete a whole different set of forms and paperwork. It's surprising Escher was Dutch and not Spanish, since dealing with officialdom here is like trying to walk up one of his staircases.

3. A total disregard of the meaning 'open' in the term 'Opening times'

Most Spanish shops, offices and businesses close between 2pm and 5pm (6pm in some areas) so that their employees can take an afternoon nap in the heat. In theory this is commendable but it was a tradition practised well before the concept of 'air conditioning'. Furthermore it's a practice that only takes place in Spain and Hispanic countries; far hotter countries seem to manage quite well without it. The Spanish call this a 'siesta'. I call it laziness. (See point 4)

4. The concept of *mañana*

Frustratingly for visitors, there's no precise definition of *mañana*; all it means is some indefinite time in the future. It might mean later that day, tomorrow morning, tomorrow evening, next Thursday, in a month's time, next year – or in many cases, never. This languid approach to life can have very different consequences. In some cases it will just be annoying (e.g. if your hotel shower needs fixing) while in other instances it could be life threatening (e.g. if you're waiting for an ambulance).

5. The esteem in which they hold their so-called 'artists'

Spain's three most famous artists were Miró, Picasso and Dalí. Now I'm as broadminded as the next man when it comes to art but quite frankly, this is definitely a case of the Emperor's new clothes. Let's look at the evidence. I can forgive Miró for having a girl's name (Joan), but all he drew were geometric squiggles that he coloured in. For some reason Picasso believed that women had both eyes on the side of their head while Dalí thought that putting a lobster on top of a telephone was clever. Innovative, ground-breaking creative geniuses or contenders for Care in the Community support? The jury is out.

3 Useful Phrases to Use in Spain

Didn't I see you on *Crimewatch*? The one where they recreated the 1983 Brink's-MAT robbery?
¿No te veo en Alerta criminal? En el que recrearon el 1983 Brink's-MAT robo?

You may call it a traditional Andalusian gypsy dance, but to me it's just an excuse to look surly and shuffle around, banging your feet on the floor.
Puedes llamarlo una danza gitana andaluza tradicional, pero para mí es sólo una excusa para mirar hosco y barajar, golpeando los pies en el suelo.

I'm sorry to hear that your pool cleaning/gardening/hairdressing business failed, but please stop bothering me with your tale of shattered dreams.
Lamento escuchar que su limpieza de la piscina/jardinería /negocio de peluquería fallaron pero por favor dejen de molestarme con su historia de sueños rotos.

Freedom of Choice #3
Third-World Child Labour

When it comes down to it, 'sweatshop' is just a word bandied around by people who don't understand the principles of a free-market economy. And as for the word 'exploits', well you can just as easily replace this with the phrase 'provides employment for'.

With my background as a City trader and as someone well-versed in the cut-and-thrust of modern business, I'm rather taken aback by the criticism of retailers like Primark. If there was no demand for cheap clothing manufactured in cramped, noisy, dangerous factories then these shops wouldn't thrive. The fact they're really successful just proves that capitalism, the bedrock of the British eco-political system, is alive and well (unlike some of the garment workers).

Arguments In Support of Third-World Garment Factories

- They give human rights lawyers and civil rights campaigners something to do.
- It's quite glamorous telling your friends that you work in the fashion industry.
- They give children a chance to experience the work environment, preparing them for adult life (albeit an adult life in exactly the same environment).
- They help workers understand the Western notion of irony (i.e. the jogging crop tops they're sewing in unsafe, oppressive conditions actually represent vitality and health).
- If the children went to school instead of working they'd only learn about things like social injustice and discrimination. Boring!
- And if they weren't sewing garments they'd only be scavenging on landfill sites or working in poisonous smelting plants.
- Children in the UK have to be sixteen in order to work full-time. Children in Asia, India, Bangladesh, South America and Sub-Saharan Africa can become economically independent when they're six.
- And unlike a lot of UK manufacturers, there's plenty of scope for them to get paid overtime (18-hour days are quite common).
- If UK retailers had to pay workers a living wage they'd

soon be out of business and the children would be out of work.

- Who are we to impose Western concepts like toilet breaks and rest periods on different cultures?
- Few workers have to take time off due to injury; the workplace accidents are such that they tend to die.
- Productivity is kept high since there's no need for workers to waste time on health and safety training…
- …and no need for factory owners to spend time on ethical compliance audits.
- They prop up the indigenous padlock industry (there are an awful lot of fire escapes that need chaining up).

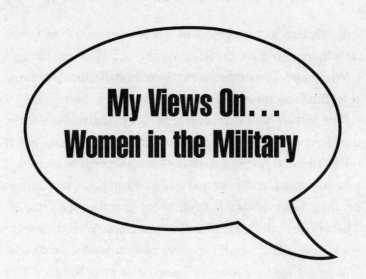

My Views On...
Women in the Military

Just like the machine-gun toting Bosch at the Battle of the Somme, the Coalition has decimated our armed forces, cutting swathes through their ranks due to forced redundancies. We used to have a world-class army; one that could keep the peace, protect our freedom and fight the fuzzy-wuzzies. Cutbacks mean that now we have less of an armed force and more of a militia. It's bloody shameful when you think that even Mexico has a much bigger army than us. Mexico! A country best known for fighting poverty and diarrhoea rather than foreign insurgents.

You probably know that UKIP policy is to not just restore our armed forces' strength but to ensure that they have the best mission-critical equipment, and that all veterans are well-looked after on their return. What I have an issue with, though, is the subject of women in the armed forces. Supporters say that modern warfare is less about physical strength and women are better suited intellectually to some roles but I still have strong reservations.

The first is about combat readiness. I'm married so I know how long my wife takes to sort out her hair and make-up. It doesn't bear thinking about how long women soldiers will take to apply khaki-coloured nail varnish, paint camouflage on their faces, or decide what boots go with their fatigues. Then there's the issue of military secrecy. Women love to gossip and it'll be hard for them to stop sending texts like, *'Guess who's getting ready to launch a surprise bombardment at 03.00. LOL! ;-)'*

And everyone knows how emotionally fragile women are. Most scream at the sight of a spider; they'll positively wet their knickers when an IED detonates. They're also not that mechanically minded. If their tank or armoured car breaks down their first instinct will be to call the AA or their husband, which is not very practical in the middle of a sustained mortar attack. Also, wars today rely far more on technology, and keyboards are often just as important as rifles. All it takes is for a long false-nail to mistype a map reference and the consequences could be disastrous.

But the biggest worry is that the presence of women can cause heightened sexual tension among male soldiers. Whether it's a traffic warden, a nurse or a schoolgirl, many men find a woman in uniform a huge turn-on and they'll probably be distracted from their usual duties and compromise a successful military operation. I don't know about you but I couldn't take that risk.

Nigel's Puzzle Page

Politics is a tough old game. After a showing my face at the European Parliament for a few hours a week I'm absobloodylutley worn out. To relax I like a pint and a puzzle. It's a great combination to take your mind off the stresses of being an MEP. Here are a few brainteasers to help yourself de-stress.

1. Ethnic Slur Search

Hidden in the square on the following page are eight names that you'll find me using (in private, of course) for some of our European neighbours. These names can be horizontal, vertical or diagonal and can read forwards or backwards.

Dago   Kraut   Polack
Frog   Wop   Fritz
Spic   Greaseball

L	S	Y	J	L	F	Q	M	N	D
L	P	M	M	P	L	R	F	T	B
A	I	B	N	N	L	R	I	Y	N
B	C	N	M	L	O	Z	K	T	K
E	F	R	O	G	L	D	K	C	Z
S	G	O	J	P	Z	J	A	Y	L
A	Z	M	G	T	K	L	P	O	W
E	B	Z	Y	A	O	R	J	V	R
R	D	T	Q	P	D	M	A	K	M
G	Z	W	L	M	N	Y	X	U	X
T	G	X	P	Z	T	M	Y	S	T

2. The Romanians and the Hotel Room Mix-Up

Three recently-arrived Romanians check into a Dover hotel and pay £10 each for a room with the hand-out they've just received from the council. They pay the £30 to the manager and go to their room.

The manager, an honest Englishman, suddenly remembers that the room rate is only £25 and gives £5 in pound coins to the bellboy to return to the immigrants.

On the way to the room the bellboy realises that £5 would be difficult to share among three people so he pockets £2 and instead gives £1 back to each of the Romanians.

That means each Romanian paid £10 and got £1 back. So they paid £9 each, totalling £27. The bellboy has the £2 he kept, totalling £29.

Where is the missing £1?

3. Foreign Aid Cock-Up

Against the wishes of the British electorate the Coalition agreed to send £70 million of foreign aid to Sudan, money that added to the UK's legacy of debt and which the Sudanese certainly did not deserve.

The Foreign Office issued what they thought were two international bank transfers for £50 million, but in actual fact some dozy, unaccountable civil servant instead sent two transfers of £100 million.

The Sudanese Finance Minister, who was equally inept, didn't notice either. He sent back to the Foreign Office what he thought were three transfers of £10 million, but which were actually three transfers of £50 million.

Who ended up better off than they should have been?

4. Bureaucracy Maze

You're a small business selling digital products when you're suddenly aware of the new EU cross-border VAT regulations on e-books, online courses and downloads that came into effect on 1 January 2015 – rules that were created by people with absolutely no understanding nor interest in how small businesses operate, nor the huge administrative burden the regulations now impose.

See if you can successfully navigate your way through the new ruling.

IN

OUT

Answers

To be honest I'm not sure. You know I'm not that good on detail. Work them out for yourself.

My Views On...
Working Mothers

Whoever said that 'A woman's place is in the home' was half-right. He should have added, 'as long as she's not getting 52 weeks Statutory Maternity Pay for sitting on her arse doing nothing'. Then that phrase would make more sense.

Look, I'm not objecting to women getting up the duff per se, but what gives them the God-given right to have paid leave as well as the opportunity to waltz right back into their old jobs – selfishly stopping under-qualified school leavers from getting their first job? My critics say that women returning to the workplace benefit their employer. They are so wrong.

Where shall I start? Well, firstly, working mums usually turn up with their baby before they're meant to return to work, disrupting employees who feel duty bound to smile and coo even though they don't really give a toss. Not only that, but this wanton flaunting of their baby can upset and cause distress to infertile women, in some cases causing them to take time off work due to depression, which further affects productivity.

It gets worse when they actually return to work. Their framed baby photos distract the women while their milk-engorged breasts distract the men (and lesbians). Then there's the extensive time off when their baby exhibits the first signs of colic, cradle cap or croup. Also, they might get a spontaneous attack of the Baby Blues, causing them to break down and wail uncontrollably in the middle of an important presentation. And if they've had a Caesarean, it means that someone else has to lift those six boxes of photocopier paper and put them away in the stationery cupboard, taking them away from their own duties. Finally, there's a good chance that technology would have moved on apace in their year off work, so they'll have absolutely no idea how to use the latest version of Windows or whatever will have taken over from email.

So, a message to any employers reading this book: if you want disruption, a drastic loss of productivity and someone practising pelvic floor exercises when they should be reconciling VAT receipts, then by all means, employ ladies of child-bearing age.

I used to dismiss the peoples of Lesotho, Swaziland and Papua New Guinea as being primitive, savage and uneducated.

That was until I found out those countries don't offer paid maternity leave.

Who's uncivilised now?